Praise for *The Unexpected Power of Home*

"If you long to make your home a gathering place where love, faith, hospitality, and joy are experienced by your family and friends, read this book. *The Unexpected Power of Home* is powerfully written and will give you fresh ideas for making your house a home. It's the perfect gift for a newly married couple or for anyone who is entering a new season of life. Nancie Carmichael writes with wisdom, depth, and tenderness. The questions at the end of each chapter make this book ideal for small group discussions or for personal use. Don't miss it!"

– Carol Kent,
Speaker and Author
He Holds My Hand: Experiencing God's Presence and Protection

"I found a sense of home in Nancie Carmichael's book, because it insightfully explains why my home is such a sanctuary for me. In *The Unexpected Power of Home* she weaves memoir and reflective insight with practical ideas to transform a home into a sacred space where families can make daily life and special occasions meaningful and memorable. Today's virtual culture connects us instantly, but what we truly need is a sense of safety and purpose and acceptance and tradition that only home provides.

Carmichael writes that we are all refugees needing a place of refuge and restoration, a place where we can learn and then give. Another insight is that our home is rooted deeply in our identity, which takes time to grow and eventually blossom. A home should be an offering to a society hungry for connection and belonging. Carmichael is right that home is powerful, because it embraces us and can fill us what we need most: love."

— Janet Holm McHenry,
Author of 23 books including
The Complete Guide to the Prayers of Jesus* and the best-selling *Prayer Walk: Becoming a Woman of Prayer, Strength, and Discipline

"We can often take home for granted, until we do not have one; trauma enters home, or we need to locate to another home. Nancie is a masterful wordsmith, and her writing draws our heart home—home the precious way God intended for us. No matter where you live, Nancie gives you the tools to build—or rebuild—a home you will look forward to living in, ministering from, and coming home to! Nancie Carmichael's beautiful sentiments, biblical wisdom, and practical insights will help you aspire to build, create, and maintain a home hearts want to dwell in, souls can grow up in, and people will love to be invited into. *The Unexpected Power of Home* is the blueprint for a safe, serene, and sanctified place where love can live."

— Pam Farrel,
author of 45 books including bestselling
Men Are Like Waffles, Women Are Like Spaghetti* and *A Couple's Journey with God

"Nancie Carmichael speaks powerfully to the longing every one of us experiences, to find (or return) to a safe place where we are known and loved—and where we belong. While acknowledging that home isn't always all that it should be, she gently challenges each of us to take the initiative to create a safe, sheltering place for ourselves and those we love, even as we look forward to the love, joy, and peace that await us in our eternal home."

– Christin Ditchfield,
internationally syndicated radio host,
conference speaker, and author of
What Women Should Know
About Letting It Go

"It is said that our story begins at home. If that is true, then there is obviously great power in the home—both the one we had and the one we make. Thus, I was absolutely delighted to discover that favorite author Nancie Carmichael has written a both practical and spiritual book—*The Unexpected Power of Home*, showing how the two intersect in life. *"We have choices when it comes to making a home, and we can take materials that we have been given to make something beautiful and good. We have choices about our lives, to make them beautiful and good too."* Her words encourage us to know ourselves and build the home atmosphere that reflects our great values. Carmichael believes that *"until we are truly at home with who we are, we continuously struggle to be at home in any place."* As she deftly takes us on a journey through the places and people in her own life, we discover that Home truly is a basic desire. *"We all long for that actual, physical place of refuge; a place of restoration and a place out of which to grow and learn and give."* *The Unexpected Power of Home* provides just that for the reader—a launching pad out into a world of discovery and purpose. Through memoir, exquisite quotes, and practical application, Carmichael is a master host in welcoming each of us into a dwelling that fits perfectly. Highly recommended wisdom for every wanderer."

– Lucinda Secrest McDowell,
author of *Dwelling Places* and *Ordinary Graces*

"I thoroughly enjoyed Nancie Carmichael's new book, *The Unexpected Power of Home.* Home is much bigger than a nicely decorated place to live. Home powerfully creates an environment of safety, comfort, security, and connection for those who live there as well as those who visit. Without home, children as well as adults will not flourish.

In our busy culture that values productivity and achievement, the importance of home is often overlooked. For those in destructive or abusive relationships, home feels more like a concentration camp or a prison environment. Home is not safe, nor secure. Nancie's book is a wake-up call for individuals and the Church to the power of home and the importance of home for now and for future generations. We must take heed."

– Leslie Vernick,
relationship coach, speaker, and
author of seven books including
The Emotionally Destructive Relationship
and *The Emotionally Destructive Marriage*

"I love home and I love this book! *The Unexpected Power of Home* is a beautiful mix of the spiritual and practical. Nancie brilliantly describes how important home is... spiritually, practically, and emotionally and gives practical suggestions how to make your home feel safe, warm, and inviting for you, your family, and friends: a comfortable chair...a favorite picture...a family meal...a place for yourself and a spot to spend time with the Lord. These things help make home feel like 'home.'"

– Lila Pearson,
interior designer and home specialist

"In *The Unexpected Power of Home,* Nancie Carmichael weaves a beautiful tapestry that—as all tapestries—celebrates warmth, artistry, strength, durability, and purpose of Home. Drawing from her own experiences with finding, leaving, and relocating home, stories of others who created homes from scraps, and a stirring collection of wisdom to line the walls of a home-hungry heart, Nancie invites us into the pages. Once there, she invites us to sit with her, rest our feet on her coffee table, and enjoy conversation about this power-packed concept. Full of opportunities for reflection as well as practical helps for weaving our own tapestries."

– Cynthia Ruchti,
writer and producer of the
long-running radio broadcast
"The Heartbeat of the Home" and
author of more than 20 books,
including *As My Parents Age* and the
novel *Miles from Where We Started*

"Nancie Carmichael had me at 'Chapter One – Home: Where Your Story Begins.' Her words caused me to reflect on my childhood home and add…'But Your Story Doesn't Have to Stop There.' That thought is made clear throughout this book. Each chapter overflows with significant reflections, guidance, and encouragement. I found myself nodding in agreement and making note of the many friends and family members who would enjoy reading *The Unexpected Power of Home.*"

– Kendra Smiley,
speaker, radio host, and
author of several books including
her latest, ***Mother of the Year – 365 Days of Encouragement for Devoted Moms***

The Unexpected Power *of* HOME

WHY WE NEED IT MORE THAN EVER

BY
NANCIE CARMICHAEL

Deep River BOOKS

The Unexpected Power of Home

Published by Deep River Books
Sisters, Oregon
www.deepriverbooks.com

ISBN - 13: 9781632694959
Library of Congress: 2018951012

First Edition–2018
Printed in the USA

27 26 25 24 23 22 21 20 19 18 10 9 8 7 6 5 4 3 2 1

Cover design by Jason Enterline
Cover Illustration by Gwendolyn Babbitt Designs

Dedication

To my children. And to Bill—who makes everything possible.

I made a home for you, my darlings. It wasn't perfect—or even close—but I gave it my best shot. Over the years I have come to believe that home is powerful, and we need it more than ever.

In making a home for you, I used material from my own childhood home and from your father's, as well as from observing my friends and extended family's homes. And yes, I used material gained from watching you! Now you are making homes of your own, and you are doing it so beautifully. I learned on the fly, by trial and error, just as you are doing. In making our homes, we can do something extraordinarily wonderful. We take the materials that we have been given, use what we value, put our own touches on it—and make it ours.

When you were small, you may have thought that even though you would grow up and leave, Home would stay, and you would return to it . . . someday. Now I see you making homes for yourselves and your own families, which is how you finally do go home again.

Welcome back.

"We were together. I forgot the rest."

– Walt Whitman

Contents

Introduction

It is said that what's most personal is most universal, and home—such an ordinary place, common to us all—may be our most personal place. I wrote this book a year and a half ago during a tumultuous time of life for us, as my husband and I sold our beloved family gathering place (too quickly, I thought), then had to scramble to find a new place.

As we looked for a new home that would work for us, I thought back over the many homes I have known: My childhood place in Montana, and what it meant to leave there, and ultimately the long winding journey to find my own home. I began writing about my persistent search for home and discovered new things. Places shape us, for good and not so good, and so it is with home, our most personal place.

We focus a lot of time and energy on where we live—whether it's an apartment, a house, an RV, or even a boat. The cost is beside the point; what matters is that it is ours and that it works for us. Our home becomes our comfort zone as we surround ourselves with our people and our things. As the old saying goes, "Be it ever so humble, there's no place like home."

What is the power of home, and why are we surprised by it? The power of home is what you do with it. Home has the potential to do much good, but it also has the power to wound. Or maybe worse—to not challenge, to waste the potential that it could have.

Home is also a place of profound self-expression, a place where we can explore and disclose who we are as we live our ordinary, wonderful lives. This too is the power of home: it is (or it can be) a picture of our inner lives, and so it is both a powerful place and an instructive place.

This book is an invitation to you: to remember the homes of your past, to shape the home of your present, and to take a deeper look at your life. Each chapter is designed to help you do these things, exploring the familiar with a new intentionality so that you can experience the power of home to its utmost.

This is a practical book. My deepest wish is that it will inspire you to take another look at your home, to see with fresh eyes what a potentially powerful place it is, despite all its complexities and challenges. When you have a home, you have the power to influence and change lives. Through your home, you have the power to create an atmosphere of safety; of beauty; of hospitality and creativity. You can create sacred, sheltering places. I pray that through this book, you will catch a fresh vision of the miraculous and unexpected power that your home offers.

While this is a practical book, it is also a spiritual book. As I studied and thought about home, I have seen that the whole concept of "home" has a higher meaning, a holiness. Home is humble; it is common; and yet we can learn wisdom from it if we pay attention, as home is also a powerful metaphor for our lives. We have choices when it comes to making a home, and we can take the materials we have been given to make something beautiful and good. We have choices about our lives, to make them beautiful and good, too.

Home is the place that grounds us. And in the end, we're all just trying to get home again.

At the end of each chapter I have included discussion questions that can facilitate a small study group, or you can use them as a personal guide to discover more about your home, and in the process, about yourself. The reflection questions are important to help open your thinking about your own home, and I hope you will use them.

Thank you for embarking on this journey with me. Let me know your thoughts and your insights through my website or Facebook page. There is so much to learn!

"Every journey brings you back home
and to yourself."

– Marty Rubin

—Nancie Carmichael
nanciecarmichael.com
Facebook.com/nancie.carmichael

CHAPTER 1

Home: Where Your Story Begins

"There are places we all come from – deep-rooty-common places – that make us who we are. And we disdain them or treat them lightly at our peril. We turn our backs on them at the risk of self-contempt. There is a sense in which we need to go home again – and can go home again.

Not to recover home, no. But to sanctify memory."[1]

We all start out somewhere. And whether we realize it or not, our earliest home has a profound influence on the way we craft our future home – what we do there and what it looks like. What do you remember of your childhood home – the people in it, as well as the actual place?

My story began on the northern windswept plains of Montana, where I was one of Harriet and Gunder Pearson's seven children. The rambling, wood-framed house where I grew up stretched to accommodate a growing family. We were "Mom-Dad-Janie-Johnny-Nancie-Judy-Danny-Kitty-Joe," my singsong mantra as I counted out places for setting the table.

My childhood home was not perfect, but it was good. Really good. Hearing others' childhood stories of hardship and strife, I feel almost apologetic that I was privileged to grow up where and when I did. Maybe the years have softened the memories and made things seem better than they actually were. Still, I look back with gratitude at the home I shared with my family under the Big Sky.

We do not get to choose our earliest home, our heartwood. Like the dense inner rings of a tree, heartwood is sturdy stuff, stubbornly strong material for which we may be forever grateful or forever resentful. But while we don't get to choose it, we do get to choose how we respond to it.

A friend of mine tells me that she doesn't have happy childhood memories. In place of those, she remembers a lot of tension between her parents. "I just remember everything at home was about not making Dad mad. We never knew which Dad would show up at home—the nice Dad or the angry Dad."

It's heartwood. But she hasn't built more of the same with it. With the perspective of years, my friend has intentionally chosen to have the kind of home she always craved—a place of consistent peace and warmth for her own three children.

As I look back on my own childhood home, I see that it was bigger than a house. My home was a house of sky, a place close to the earth and shaped by the seasons. It was not a perfect home. I resisted my father's stubborn sense of legalism in living a holy life. (Why couldn't we have a TV? Why was he so strict about not wearing makeup? No movies! No dancing! No fun.) In spite of that, I had a sense he was protecting us as best as he knew how.

My childhood home lies ten miles north and three miles east of Conrad, Montana, on what they call the North Bench. It sits above the Marias River near where Meriweather Lewis tangled with the Blackfeet Indians in 1806. I know I am getting close to home when I turn off the highway onto a graveled road. From a mile or so away, I can see the unmistakable silhouette of our barn, built in the late 1800s, still sturdy today. The house itself is surrounded by clumps of ash and cottonwood trees and is painted white. When you get closer, you can see the pink and white peonies and the front-yard lilac bushes my mother planted years ago. The flowers are still there, but both of my parents are gone, and my brother Dan and his growing family now own the place.

My father, Gunder, was a cattle and wheat rancher on land where you can see the snow-covered Rocky Mountains off to the west; and off to the northeast, the Sweet Grass Hills of Alberta. Some days the mountains look startlingly close; some days they are distant and hazy. When Gunder came to visit us in Oregon, he felt hemmed in by the trees. "I like to see," he said. And he sure could see from our place in Montana, for miles and miles off to the distant mountains.

Except for the summer, our lives were dictated by the rhythms of the one-room country school across the street from our house. There were about a dozen students, half of whom were my brothers and sisters.

I was a skinny tomboy with a tangled mess of blonde hair who loved being outside every spare minute, no matter the season, climbing trees, playing in the barn. In the winter, the air was so cold that it hurt to breathe, and the snow sparkled like diamonds, so you had to shield your eyes to look. In the tenuous springtime, meadowlarks would sing mornings and evenings on the fence behind our house or sway from the tops of cattails in the ditch along the road. Summer brought the scent of lilacs in our front yard and of the earth softening, of things growing. On hot summer afternoons, rolling thunderstorms would race across the sky to dump rain and sometimes hail upon the parched earth. We children would run into the house before the crashing lightning came too close and stand at the screen door, mesmerized.

Each of us experiences home in a unique and complex way. It is an ever-changing dynamic, hard to define. Siblings from the same parents can have entirely different memories of growing up, of what "home" meant. And even good memories can bring pain, because the people and the places are no more, or have changed. Some of us just need to get over a happy childhood. As Dr. Seuss advised, "Don't cry that it's over. Smile that it happened."[2]

"The past is not dead, it is living in us, and will be alive in the future which we are now helping to make."[3]

Why look back?

Why is it important to reflect on your childhood home?

We look back to see the truth of our story, to understand what shaped us. The psalmist wrote, "You desire truth in the inward parts, and in the hidden part, you will make me to know wisdom."[a] It is in the inward part of us, where we are most truthful about our own story,

[a] Psalm 51:6, NKJV

that we can gain wisdom and understanding. We learn what to treasure, what to keep. What to let go. We learn how to build a beautiful and good home because we are informed by wisdom. A proverb says, "Through wisdom a house is built, and by understanding it is established; by knowledge the rooms are filled with all precious and pleasant riches."[b]

Remembering arms us with truth and wisdom.

What were the sounds of your childhood home?

When we are young, our senses are keen. The past can come alive for us again as we remember the sounds . . . the smells . . . the touches . . . the tastes . . . the sights of home. What do you remember of your earliest home? As you think back to the sounds of your childhood home, it may surprise you what memories you uncover.

My childhood home was noisy. My uncles and neighbors often dropped in, which meant the deep rumble of men's voices as they discussed the crops and the weather to the clink of spoons in coffee cups. There was the sound of my siblings playing, arguing. Quiet moments only came for me when I went outside, which was a lot. I usually had a secret place—a place to be by myself, to write, to read. Sometimes it was in the barn, or if it was summer, in the trees behind our house. We didn't have a television, as Gunder didn't approve of such worldly intrusions, so we found ways to entertain ourselves.

In the winter, the boys played whirlwind games of basketball in their bedroom, accompanied by shouts and

---

[b] Proverbs 24:3,4, NKJV

slams against the door. Or they rigged up the dining room table to play ping-pong, and I'd hear the ball dashing back and forth to the slap of the paddle. I remember the sound of my mother typing furiously on her typewriter, writing letters to my married older sister or pounding out a short story she was writing. There was often music: Nat King Cole on the stereo, or strains of gospel music from itinerant evangelists who came through, often staying at our house, whose albums we felt obligated to buy. *"I'll fly away . . ."*

Piano practice was an ever-present sound: myself, my sisters Judy and Kitty, or my brother Dan, getting ready for recitals. There was often the sound of singing, as we practiced for the duets or trios we would do at school concerts, at church, or camp meeting. It's no wonder my mother would often exclaim in exasperation, "It's so noisy in here, I can't think straight!"

In the spring, we could hear through the open window the drone of Dad's tractor in the distance, breaking up the soil to plant wheat. In March or April, the unbounded song of red-winged blackbirds migrating north filled the air with a stop in the trees behind our house. Where I live now in central Oregon, the return of the red-winged blackbird is likewise one of the first signs of spring. When I hear their frenetic song, I'm taken back to coming home from school on a March day and seeing the still-bare trees behind our house filled with blackbirds calling their crazy-joyful sound.

Chaos was my comfort zone. Our earliest experiences of home tend to become our default setting, ingraining habits and expectations of what home should look and feel—and sound—like. Now, when my family is here, and our house is full, I feel like myself again. I feel that this is the way life should be lived—in a big, noisy house with family savoring the seasons.

> *"Home. When it rains, you can smell the leaves in the forest and the sand. It's all so small and mild, the landscape surrounding the lake, so manageable. The leaves and the sand are so close, it's as if you might, if you wanted, pull them on over your head. And the lake always laps at the shore so gently, licking the hand you dip into it like a young dog, and the water is soft and shallow."*
>
> *– Jenny Erpenbeck, Visitation*

The Power of Scent

While all of our senses are powerful, perhaps the power of scent triggers more memories than any of them. There is research to suggest the olfactory bulb has direct connections to two brain areas that are strongly implicated in emotion and memory: the amygdala and the hippocampus. Interestingly, visual, auditory, and tactile information does not pass through these brain areas.[c]

My husband loves the smell of freshly sawn lumber as it reminds him of working with his builder-father on a construction site. For me, when I smell the garlicky-onion fragrance of a pot roast simmering in the oven, I remember coming home as a child Sunday mornings after

---

[c] Jordan Gaines Lewis, Ph.D, *"Smells Ring Bells: How Smell Triggers Memories and Emotions,"* posted January 12, 2015 www.psychologytoday.com/blog/brain-babble/201501/smells-ring-bells, accessed 2/23/2018

church and walking in the door, feeling faint with hunger. It seemed an eternity for my mother to mash the potatoes and make the gravy.

The smell of oregano or basil reminds me of the fine day when I was about ten and our engaging and entertaining pastor, Gil Mandigo (who had some Italian in him), came out to the farm. We all got in the kitchen and made something radically new: pizza pie. Mother made the crust, and we all got involved with this novel dish, adding tomato sauce, herbs, cheese, and toppings. From then on, we were hooked on pizza.

The smell of good food means hospitality to me, and a constant stream of people dropped in at my parents' home for coffee or a meal. People need food, after all. On Sundays, it might be a visiting preacher or missionary or some singing group. My aunts from California, whom my dad called "the girls," came in the summer. Our house was their home when they first moved to Montana from North Dakota. It never occurred to me as a child that our home used to belong to someone else. I can only imagine the memories that flooded Evelyn and Alice when they too left the highway and drove down the graveled road to see their home place.

When Uncle Kenny, my mother's brother, and his wife, Aunt Julia, would arrive with our cousins from North Dakota, we children would be giddy to see them and would immediately head for the barn or somewhere to play outside while my mother's huckleberry pie cooled on the counter. We knew that after dinner, there would be pie and coffee along with jokes and old stories told and retold, and much laughter.

Occasionally Harriet, my mother, would go on a cleaning frenzy and not stop until everything gleamed, and she felt free to drop into her chair and sip her coffee that had grown cold. In between the cleaning frenzies (usually precipitated by *"Company's coming!"),* she was more relaxed—working a crossword puzzle or badgering us to play Scrabble with her. Harriet loved poetry and would often stop what she was doing, and with a dreamy look, begin to quote a line from Shakespeare or Tennyson. While she sewed clothes for us, her canary, Larry Bird, would sing along with the sewing machine.

I will never forget the pungent smell of chemicals as our kitchen also doubled as a salon, as my mother would give perms and haircuts to women in the community. Before she married, she had worked in a beauty salon. Hers were highly valued skills in a rural community!

Some smells bring not-so-great memories. One of my jobs as a girl was to help take care of the chickens, and the distinctive musty smell of the chicken coop and flying feathers (especially when the coop was overdue to be shoveled out) makes me glad I haven't embraced the mini-chicken-coop-in-your-backyard revival. After gathering eggs, I would have to wash the chicken manure off, crate the eggs, and take them into the local grocery. And those handsome ceramic roosters people buy to put on their gleaming kitchen counters? I just don't see the romance of it. You may have some negative memories associate with certain smells from your childhood too. Whatever the associations, positive or negative, take the time to think through your memories of home.

The people in your homes

> *"Children need more than food, shelter, and clothing. The bottom line is: Every child needs at least one person who's crazy about him."*[4]

Without doubt, home is a place. But it's also people. We provide our people and our children with a place and then surround them with who we are.

My mother Harriet's smile was like sunshine, and it warmed everyone in her path. She was the youngest in her Canadian family, and like many youngest children, she was funny. Her father had been in Vaudeville, so Harriet learned a streak of comedic humor that served her well in life on the northern plains.

Gunder, handsome, blue-eyed, and good to the bone, was the hardworking son of Swedish immigrants. His father was a Lutheran pastor in North Dakota. My father took Jesus' call to visit the poor and sick literally, and he often dragged us reluctant children along on his errands of mercy.

Gunder was a taciturn, steady presence in our home. When he wasn't working on the farm, he was teaching Sunday School, picking up kids who needed a ride to church, or going to one of many board meetings somewhere. He never passed up a hitchhiker. He quite literally "went about doing good" in the community, and he wanted us children to be good too, to serve the Lord. (He often pleaded with me and my sister to go along with him to visit shut-ins or those who were down on their luck. I was to play my accordion, and we both would sing for them. We went along with his request, but I can't imagine that my accordion music alleviated anyone's suffering.) He wanted us to do well in school, take piano lessons, work hard, go to college, and make something of ourselves. He set a high bar.

Our farm was organic and free-range long before anyone had heard of such things. Self-sustaining was not a hobby, it was survival. We guarded water for personal use carefully, as Gunder had to haul it from town until a few years later when we were finally able to hook up to water from Tiber Dam. Before that, Harriet had to wash clothes using a wringer washer in the bunkhouse and hang clothes to dry on a clothesline. I still savor the scent of sheets fresh from outside. In the winter, clothes were hung on racks inside. It was a constant battle for my mother to keep the outside *out,* and in the summer, she fought to keep dirt, flies, and mosquitoes out of the house. I remember the sound of the screen door slamming as we children would come and go. Grandma, who came to the farm every weekend to help my mother, would say, "Make up your mind: either stay in or stay out!"

Our lives were ordered by the seasons. Planting; tilling; harvesting. Taking care of the cattle was a continual responsibility. In the summer, we would help our mother pick plums and crab apples to make jelly and jams.

I am struck by the strong sense of togetherness and community that I experienced as a child at home, at school, the church and 4-H. We revered our teacher, Mr. Schwoch, who taught us to love books and poetry. When we children weren't playing together or at school, we worked alongside our parents. Life was simple and full.

"The people who influence us most
are not those who buttonhole us and talk to us,
but those who live their lives like the stars in heaven
and the lilies in the field, perfectly simply and
unaffectedly. Those are the lives that mold us."

– Oswald Chambers

About those grandparents . . .

"It's important to honor your ancestors. Bringing in a piece of furniture or an object you've inherited from a loved one not only honors the person who has passed but also brings the warmth of happy memories into your home."[5]

What do you remember of your grandparents? Grandparents are powerfully important, and their influence reaches us even if we didn't know them.

I only knew my mother's mother, Grandma Olson, as the others passed away years before I got on the scene. Maud Anna Davis Olson was an integral part of our family: a strong presence and a whirlwind of energy. She lived in an apartment in Conrad, a town thirteen miles from us, but she often came out on the weekends to help. And help she did. She planted the garden and did the wash, both major jobs. She was not an indulgent grandmother, and I often felt that she vaguely disapproved of me. She cracked the whip and Got Things Done. One day when I was a little girl, I was with her at the post office in Conrad and the clerk greeted her, "Good morning, Grandma!" She gave him a steely look and replied, "I'm not your grandma."

It wasn't until I grew older that I gained more understanding of my grandmother. Dark-eyed and snappy Maud was from a staunchly Welsh family with roots deep in Minnesota and the Midwest. She married John Olson in 1904 in Minnesota. John and Maud soon moved back to Saskatchewan near John's parents, which is where my mother was born, the youngest of four. But hard times visited John and Maud. The Great Depression was difficult enough, but on top of it, John had what was then called a nervous breakdown, and after many years, died in a mental institution in Saskatchewan. Unfortunately, in those days there was little treatment for mental illness, and Maud was left to fend for herself and her four children any way she could. She stayed with her in-laws in Saskatchewan until Harriet was born. After that, she embarked upon a vagabond existence, following work in Montana or North Dakota, doing what she could to make a living.

My mother's two older sisters died early in life. Occasionally when Mother would talk of her sisters, she would cry for them. "Death is the final enemy," Harriet would say, wiping her eyes.

It's no wonder Grandma Olson wasn't a warm and fuzzy person. She had to be tough to survive. She lived by her wits and sheer hard work, cleaning houses, cleaning men's suits, babysitting and cooking for harvesters. I believe the hard work she did to support herself and her family gave her a sense of dignity and purpose as she provided home along the way, even in the most difficult of times.

"Voices call from unseen rooms
Echoing down the empty hall
Beckoning us to enter into
Worlds yet to be explored.
Sister, brother, parent, child,
Singing in the blood, singing in the bone,
Remember me, Remember me"

– Michael E. Williams

As a child, I did not know the stories of my father's parents. "Tell me, Dad," I'd beg my father. "Tell me about your family, your parents. Your early childhood."

"Well, there isn't much to tell," he'd say. Not true. There was a lot to tell. But my father's way of dealing with a painful past was to repress it.

I began digging for information about my grandparents and discovered accounts my aunt Evelyn had written of their early years. Ancestry.com told the record of the family's immigration as well as their births, marriages, and deaths. I also spoke to an old family friend who knew my father's people, and bit by bit, I pieced together their story.

Henney and Gabriel Pearson, my father's parents, emigrated separately from Sweden and met at the Lutheran Church in Bemidji, Minnesota, where he was a student pastor. They married in Minot, North Dakota, in 1909. Gabriel and Henney went to seminary in St. Peters, Minnesota, at Gustavus Adolphus College, and Gabriel became a Lutheran pastor in Lignite, North Dakota. My husband and I visited the seminary not long ago and found their names in a dusty old book of early alumni, high on a shelf in their library. It's unclear whether or not Henney actually attended the school as a student; regardless, her name was listed along with Gabriel's. It seemed that she was a full partner in ministry with her husband.

I was delighted to finally have a small connection with the grandparents I never knew. I bought a sweatshirt in the college bookstore with *Gustavus Adolphus* emblazoned on it, in memory of them. They were real people. They had lived in real places. Some pieces of the puzzle that was my paternal grandparents slipped into place, adding to my own concept of "home."

Gabriel built his growing family a big home on a lake, and we are told Henney was a charming woman, a great housekeeper and cook, and always open to company coming.

Gabriel and Henney must have had such high hopes for their new life in America, for their family, for their ministry. None of those plans would take shape. Gabriel died at age thirty-nine from a ruptured appendix. Henney was six months pregnant with her sixth child, my aunt Emma. A few years later, Henney remarried and had three more children. Then tragedy struck again as her second husband, Edward Anderson, died of a sudden illness. Henney died not long after that at age forty-four, of cancer, leaving nine children orphaned.

Incredibly, the family stuck together. The older children took care of the younger children, ages twenty-two to two. Evelyn became the surrogate mother and Bernhard the surrogate father. Neither ever had children of their own.

One catastrophe after another struck the nine orphaned children. The Depression hit, along with the damage of a drought. The family auctioned everything off in 1937 and moved to Montana. I cannot imagine their sense of loss. But somehow, they pulled together and looked forward to rebuilding their lives. With the heartwood they had been given from Gabriel and Henney—that of faith in God, of hard work and stubborn resilience—they began the work of making new homes in a new place.

After they moved to Montana and my father married my mother, tragedy again struck the family when the youngest—the baby of the family, Raymond—was killed in an accident driving a truck. He was only eighteen years old. The family again was devastated.

> *"Home is where one starts from. As we grow older The world becomes stranger, the pattern more complicated."*
>
> *—T.S. Eliot, Four Quartets, East Coker 1940*

Stories converge

My father's family knew more death, more tragedy, than most. But the life force goes on. Young people seek to build a home, make their own way, pursue their own dreams. They look for and find love.

In 1945, my father's story converged with my mother's. The vivacious, auburn-haired Harriet Olson was a single mother who worked in a beauty salon in Great Falls, Montana, where she lived with her mother, Maud, and Harriet's daughter, Hattie Jayne. (*The Place of Belonging,*[6] written by Jayne Pearson Faulkner, gives a moving account of her and Harriet's early life.)

One spring Sunday, my father happened to visit the Great Falls church where my mother attended, and that is where they met and fell in love. In October of 1945, Gunder Pearson and Harriet Olson married to make a new home.

You can say all you want to about people and places not defining you, but they do. Along with that, you are forever marked by certain life-altering events in your life, be the marks unseen or seen. They are there. My father's life was marked by loss. The Depression, illness, and cancer devastated his family. My mother's rootless life of surviving, of finding love but being abandoned and left to be a single mother in the late 1930s, had to be difficult. Shame stalked her. And yet there are second chances. God offers mercy and restoration, and both of my parents found faith in God. And they found each other.

While nobody wants adversity, it forges character. Through it, people have the opportunity to learn self-reliance, survival skills, and commitment to important principles. I wonder what stressors and cultural influences are shaping us now, shaping our homes. When we are immersed in the present, we often do not see what is affecting us. Technology and isolation and materialism are ever-present, all forces that might war against the formation of our homes—but we can consciously make our homes good, healing places for all those who enter. My parents somehow took their broken homes and put them together to make a whole one: a place of joy and purpose in which their children thrived.

> *"I wonder if ever again Americans can have that experience of returning to a home place so intimately known, profoundly felt, deeply loved, and absolutely*

> *submitted to? It is not quite true that you can't go home again. I have done it, coming back here. But it gets less likely. We have had too many divorces. We have consumed too much transportation, we have loved too shallowly in too many places."*[7]

At a recent family reunion, my family and I shared stories and laughed until our sides hurt as we watched slides, snapshots of the past and present. My nephew built a fire pit, and later that evening we sat around it, talking about shared memories. As I looked at dear faces gathered, I thought, *This is so ancient, and yet so present. The elders and the young ones sitting around the campfire, telling stories.* "And we speak of our Patriarch Abraham. And Sarah. And we tell of Moses crossing the Red Sea." That is how much of the Bible was written—as stories told, passed down orally around campfire and hearth fire, passed into writing.

And so we tell of Maud Ann, who raised four children in the Great Depression, alone. And we tell of Gabriel and Henney, who left their home country for the new land, for new opportunities, only to die early, leaving their nine children to raise each other. And we tell of Gunder, and of Harriet who struggled but persevered. We tell of how they built a good home and raised children in a place of love, and trusted God even when things didn't look good.

So I'm reminded: Do what matters now. Build that home. And when you need to, leave it to build another. Because the home is for you. The home will matter now, and it will matter a generation from now.

We stand on the shoulders of those who came before us. We make our own homes from the materials that have been given to us. And while we cannot choose the circumstances of our early lives, we can choose what to remember. We can choose to use the good material we have been given to build our own homes. We can also choose not to incorporate the negative. And while we are living our own story, we can tell our story to our children, to those who come after us. We are witnesses to our own unique story.

When I left my childhood home for college in the fall of 1965, I thought home would always be there—that it would always be a place ready to welcome me back. But home is elusive. Although it may center on a fixed place, it is also a constantly changing place that contains us, that supports who we are. And as we change, so home must change.

When I was seventeen and packing to go to college in Southern California with my older brother John, I remember sitting out under the trees behind our house thinking, *I love this place, but I'm leaving it.* I had no idea where life would take me. Just that something inside was saying, *There's more out there. It's time to go.*

I had no idea of the twists and turns ahead. Of the many places I would go. Marriage, having babies, working with my husband were all ahead of me. And all along the way, I would look to make a home to support our life.

And always, in the back of my mind, I thought that I would go home again, someday. I would.

"Softly and tenderly Jesus is calling,

Calling for you and for me;

See, on the portals He's waiting and watching,

Watching for you and for me.

Come home, come home, Ye who are weary, come home;
Earnestly, tenderly, Jesus is calling,
Calling, O sinner, come home!"
– Will L. Thompson, 1847–1909

Take some time to reflect on your earliest home and jot down memories from your childhood. It may be painful; it may bring gratitude. But most of all, it may bring insight and wisdom to your life now.

If you are in a discussion group, share with others what you are learning.

Here are some questions to lead you:

- What do you remember most about the people in your earliest home?
- Who was the most fun to be with, and what made them fun?
- Who was your safest person? Your most difficult person?
- What are your earliest memories of your grandparents?
- If you did not know your grandparents, what are some ways you can discover more about them?
- As you look at your home now, what influences do you see from your grandparents? (This may take some consideration. Take the time you need to think it through!)
- Try to remember some of the sounds, smells, tastes, touches, sights of your childhood home. Describe them.
- What is your "comfort zone" in your home now? Why is that true for you?
- List two factors that made your childhood home good. How are you incorporating those qualities in your home now?
- What is one quality about your childhood home that you would change if you could?

Chapter 2

Leaving Home

"You think [that life in a small town is good] because you live in a city. Family life in a little town is pretty deadly. It's being planted in the earth, like one of your carrots here. I'd rather be pulled up and thrown away."[8]

As long as there have been homes, there has been the leaving of them.

Leaving home is like uprooting a tender young plant—pulling roots and all out of the ground—and then trying to find a place to transplant it where hopefully, in time, it will thrive.

It was late August 1965. I was seventeen and eager to leave home for college, but I was beginning to understand that this meant leaving my Montana home, and home was in every fiber of my being—the farmhouse where I'd lived all my life, the trees behind the house where I would sit with a notepad and write, all my secret places where I could escape the noise of a large family.

The little gray Studebaker was packed. I was going to college in Southern California with my older brother John, which made leaving easier. He was my hero, the smartest person on earth. John was impatient to leave, and this being his sophomore year, he'd already had a taste of freedom and wanted more of it. I had checked and rechecked all my earthly belongings—clothes mainly, and a few treasured books. Where was Dad? I couldn't leave without saying good-bye.

I walked down past the barn to look for him. I found him by a granary, repairing a fence. I remember crying as I walked, saying good-bye to the trees, the barns, our Siamese cat, Cedric, and Alfie, our bouncy springer spaniel. How I loved the meadowlarks' song, the swallows wheeling in the air, the breathtaking canopy of sky—how could I leave this for California, where towns all ran into each other so that you never even knew what town you were in? A place where you didn't dare speak to strangers?

I didn't know how it was that I could do such a thing. I only knew something inside me was saying it was time to go.

"Dad. We're leaving." I reached up to hug him and saw that he too was crying.

He stood, leaning on a shovel, clad in his usual overalls, sobs shaking his shoulders. Aghast, I stopped my own crying. "Why, Dad . . ." He put his arms around me and gave me an awkward kiss, tears making rivers down his sunburned face, his Swedish blue eyes brimming. Oh, love can be a painful thing. I knew at that moment that he loved me, although he had never said so. To his thinking, there were some feelings, some emotions too big for words. And what you felt for your flesh and blood, one whose eyes mirrored yours—well, some things are impossible to say.

What can parents say at such a time as this? Maybe simply smile, wipe away the tears, and say, "Call us soon, okay? Is there enough gas in the car? Have you checked the oil? Drive carefully!" All the exit statements that parents have to say when what they want to say is, "Do you have to go so soon? Now wait . . . there was something important I had to say to you, but for the life of me, what was it? Are you really leaving, child of mine?"

Home is a powerful metaphor for our lives, a living metaphor in which we all participate. We have a home; then there's the leaving of it.

> *"To depart is to die a little. But to stay is to die a little, too . . . One must have a place before one can give it up. One must receive before giving, exist before abandoning oneself in faith. We receive a place only so as eventually to leave it, treasure only so as to cast it away, a personal existence only so as to be able to offer it up."*[9]

What do we take with us when we leave?

It's an important question. Mostly, we take ourselves and all that has gone into us up until now: our family's influence, our education, and our expectations of life. And we take actual stuff. We need furnishings, no matter how basic. In the summer before school starts, stores put up big displays marketed to college students to show them what they need for their first temporary home away from home. Sheets and comforters, mini-refrigerators and microwaves. Computers and iPads. When my sons were first setting up their college apartments, they would eye furnishings in our house. "Mom, are you using that lamp? How about that chair?"

California in the sixties couldn't have been more different from my Montana home. I realized that much quickly! I don't remember doing much studying that first semester as my roommate and I set about having fun. A lot of freedom at once had its pitfalls, and we were boy crazy. The college was near the beach, and we went there often.

In my first semester at college, I navigated a rocky relationship with a boy, and finally broke it off—the first healthy decision in the relationship on my part. By January, I wanted to get out of there. I was terribly homesick, and I'd had it with California and the college scene. I was tired of freeways, and I longed for back roads and familiar places. I called my mother and told her I wanted to come home.

I hoped she would throw the door wide open. She didn't. Mother advised me to stick it out until the end of the school year and try to make the best of my time there. When I came home for the summer, we could talk about what I should do.

Helping your children leave home

My mother was right not to immediately rescue me from my homesickness. Josh Klapow, a clinical psychologist and associate professor at the University of Alabama's School of Public Health, says that homesickness isn't necessarily about home. Rather, it stems from a need for love, protection, and security—qualities usually associated with our childhood homes. "It's normal and adaptive to feel homesick for some period of time." He and other experts advise parents on how to help their freshmen. They suggest you:

- Avoid expressing anxiety or telling your children how much you miss them
- Focus on the positive things they are experiencing
- Text to set up a good time for FaceTime
- Be excited for the new things they are experiencing
- Help them make good decisions and emphasize good life skills
- Help them with boundaries

I took my mother's advice to heart, and the next semester I did a reset. I took my classes seriously. I got involved in choir and piano and started completing assignments. The chapel was open in the evening, and it became my refuge where I could play the piano, which brought a sense of home to me.

Shortly after the second semester started, I met Bill Carmichael, a young man who was also in choir. He was twenty-three, I was eighteen. Bill had already graduated from a different college and enrolled where I attended to pursue a graduate degree in education. Bill was a music major with a lovely Irish tenor voice, and he needed an accompanist for a solo. I was happy to do it. I loved his sparkling blue eyes, his sense of humor, and his dreams to make a difference, to do something good for God and the world. I felt at home with Bill right from the start, and we loved being together, talking.

When I went back to Montana for the summer, it was with Bill—and with an engagement ring on my finger. We had a date to marry in my home church in Conrad in August and then take our first jobs as youth pastor and church secretary in San Francisco at a church near the Haight-Ashbury. That summer was a blur, culminating in a late August wedding in my home church surrounded by family and friends. The wedding was a wonderful celebration, and as we left for our honeymoon, I wondered, *How can life get any better?*

When my new husband and I returned to the farm from our honeymoon in Glacier Park to pack up and get our things, the people who made it home weren't there. Harvest was over, and while we were gone, my parents and siblings had left for North Dakota to visit relatives. The farm and the house were quiet. It was time to get on with our lives as a married couple. Bill found a small trailer in the want ads, and we loaded it with all our belongings. Evidently the wedding gift to give in the summer of 1966 was tablecloths, as we received twenty-one of them in various sizes and shapes. I had no clue what I would need to furnish my first home. I just knew I'd need some cooking utensils. I suddenly became aware that I would have to expand my recipes beyond chocolate chip cookies and green salad. My new husband liked to eat, and both he and I would need meals—*every day!* I had a lot to learn.

This time when I left home, I really left. Leaving the farm this time felt different, more final. I was a married woman now, and I planned to help Bill get through graduate school while we both worked.

Our first apartment was in an old, dilapidated building next to the church. We occupied four rooms, all identical in size: a living room, kitchen, bedroom, and bathroom. The building creaked when the wind blew around its corners. Still, to be young and in love in the city was exhilarating. We loved our work with teenagers, and our apartment was often filled with young people, many of them off the streets, runaways from home, flower children looking for love. We listened to Martin Luther King's dream speech on our tiny black-and-white TV. We went with friends to the airport to greet Bobby Kennedy on his swing through the west coast. We were alarmed about Vietnam and somehow sensed that we were living through a dynamic cultural sea change.

On our first Christmas in San Francisco, the reality of having left began to dawn on me. We didn't have enough time off from our jobs to drive back to Montana, and we couldn't afford to fly. It made me realize I wasn't ever going back home again. Not really.

We spent our first Christmas together with Bill's warm and hospitable family in Santa Cruz. But they weren't my parents; it wasn't my home; and I was homesick. I didn't know my in-laws' routines, their traditions. Leaving and cleaving didn't seem all that romantic anymore, and there were nights I cried myself to sleep. I missed my brothers and sisters, especially my sister Judy, who was closest in age to me. She was my soul mate, and we had done everything together growing up—school, music, friends. Leaving home as a married woman was like crossing a one-way bridge.

I imagine how leaving must have been for my dad's parents, Gabriel and Henney, who both left Sweden as teenagers to come to America. Henney came with her mother aboard the *Baltic* and arrived at Ellis Island in 1906.

She met Gabriel later, in Bemidji, Minnesota, at the Swedish Lutheran church. When they left Sweden, the possibility of ever seeing their loved ones again—of ever seeing their home place again—was remote. There were no non-stop flights then; no Facetime or Skype. Leaving was final. Surely both were homesick yet exhilarated at being in a new country with new possibilities as they took English classes to learn about America, the land of opportunity.

Still, my father and his siblings always carried their parents' love of the old country and its comfortable ways—the discipline of the church, the community, hard work. Certain foods. My father occasionally ordered wooden crates of pickled herring, and his eyes would light up when they arrived. On holidays, we had lutefisk, a type of boiled cod, and lefse, made from mashed potatoes, tender and delicious when buttered and spread with sugar. No doubt these tastes and smells reminded him of his mother and father and people long left behind.

When you first leave home, what do you miss most? If you're like me, it's the familiar sounds, the smells. Your own bed. Chicken enchiladas as only Mom can make them. A relaxed familiarity where you can be yourself, and the inside jokes you don't have to explain; what you laugh at and what you don't laugh at. You know where not to stub your toe in the middle of the night when you get up to go pee.

Mostly, you miss the people.

Why leave?

Why do explorers, adventurers, children, *leave?* Why do we leave home? We leave because we sense there is more, a calling that we must answer. We leave because we feel invited to the future, to independence, which is somewhere else. Our childhood home no longer defines us. It's our mother's or father's house to which we return on occasion. Leaving our childhood home is the first step to finding our own home. We leave in answer to the drive to find where we belong, beginning with a sense that "I don't fit here anymore."

It has always been this way. Abram left to seek his country, responding to God's direction: "Get out of your country, from your family and from your father's house to a land I will show you."[10] Christopher Columbus left to find passage to the East and stumbled upon the Americas.

Tisquantum (known as Squanto), a member of the Patuxet band of the Wampanoag people and a friend to the Pilgrims, was born in the Cape Cod area of Massachusetts around 1580.[11] It was his tribe's tradition that an early teen would leave his parents and tribe to survive for a winter by himself in the wilderness. When he returned home in the spring, the time alone would have proved his manhood and demonstrated that he was worthy of his place in the community as a brave.

He was only one among many who was practicing "leaving." The Pilgrims left England to come to the new country to worship freely. Captain James Cook left England in the late 1700s and sailed to civilizations yet unknown to the Europeans.[12] Everywhere, those who left also created new homes. Our own more recent history of pioneers on the Oregon Trail is well documented by stories and journals. Historian Howard Lamar and psychiatrist Daniel Levinson have suggested that pioneers who settled the western part of the United States on the "overland passage played a vital role in the life cycle of men, corresponding to 'breaking away,' improving, or bettering oneself, the stages that mark a man's life."[13]

It's interesting to note that many women pioneers went only to support their men and were themselves reluctant to leave home. It was a drastic and dangerous leaving, and most would never see their parents and home again. Many women recorded in their diaries their misgivings. Mary A. Jones wrote of her husband in 1846 that she told him, *"O let us not go."* But her pleas made no difference.[14] He was captivated by the possibilities of the new country to the west.

Statistics show the sheer courage and fortitude that it took for these early pioneers to follow the Oregon Trail. A half-million people made the two-thousand-mile trek west between 1843 and 1860. Twenty thousand of them died on the way—from cholera, typhoid, the flu, measles, or accidents. Despite the widespread fears of Indians, only 362 travelers were killed by Indians; and 426 Indians were killed by travelers.[15]

While leaving can be exciting, it takes sacrifice, no matter who or where you are. And when we leave, it impacts the ones left behind.

Ten years before I left home, I watched my older sister Janie pack to leave for college. I followed her from room to room as she put final touches on her luggage. She had a flight to catch out of Great Falls on her way to college in Missouri. I was seven, she was seventeen, and I couldn't imagine life without my big sister, who read to us by the hour. Janie made up stories that were more exciting than anything in a book, and she was always there with her patient kindness and love. I sobbed and wailed as I followed her from room to room. Finally, she stopped, bent over, and held both of my shoulders. "Please don't," she said rather severely. "It just makes it harder for me." That finally shut me up.

Shortly after our third son, Chris, left for college, Andy, our youngest son, came in the house and slammed the door. *"It's too quiet in here!"* he exclaimed. I agreed, it was too quiet. It is often too quiet for those left behind.

But when you are the one doing the leaving, you are focused on your own future, no looking back.

It's easier to leave home when you are young, because you think that home will always be there for you, and that you will go back to it. (And you will. Briefly.) It's exciting to leave, because it's a time for you to explore, to start making your own decisions. There's a big world out there. And truthfully, some leavings are gleeful on the part of both the children and the parents. I know some parents who high-five each other when their children leave.

Leaving helps you grow up

> *"The truth is that from the day we're born until the day we die, we need to feel held and contained somewhere. We can let go and become independent only when we feel sufficiently connected to other people."*[16]

As children get ready to leave home, conflict can arise. Bill says the nest just gets messy with all the wings flapping, and the clamor is a sign that it's time for somebody to go. It's time to learn a new language in a new place, the language of independence and responsibility. Leaving home sets things in motion that change us.

We feel a conflicting set of emotions—we want to leave; we want to stay. Home is comfortable, but it can swallow us up if we don't go, almost like a Venus flytrap or a mother with a big billowy lap who wants to keep you there (for your own good, of course, but you can't wait to leave . . . knowing you may want to return someday, in case it doesn't work out). Leaving is necessary to growing. Leaving equips us to make a new home, to become our own person. Letting go of home can be symbolic of letting go of our parents, our siblings, even (on the other side of life) our children. For the parents whose children fly, this can be painful.

I dug through my cedar chest for old letters of my mother's—letters she wrote me when she was the age I am now. I read them, trying to get a feel for what she was experiencing. It was hard for her too, letting her children go. She worried a lot, even though she prayed daily for us. At the time, I didn't give her feelings much thought. I was busy trying to get on with my life.

> *"In life, a person will come and go from many homes. We may leave a house, a town, a room, but that does not mean those places leave us. Once entered, we never entirely depart the homes we make for ourselves in the world. They follow us, like shadows, until we come upon them again, waiting for us in the mist."*[17]

The Cycle Continues: Our Children Leave Us

Now that I am a parent of grown children and have watched all five of my children leave home, I see that leaving is a big deal, a watershed moment. When you are the parents standing at the door waving good-bye, you finally understand your own parents. In parenting, there is so much letting go.

What a cruel hoax it is to fall hopelessly in love with your child, only to realize as the years go by that he or she is not yours after all. All the years of sleepless nights; of sometimes ordinary, sometimes exhilarating days; of countless meals and laundry, training, school, sports, teaching them the best you can to love God in the midst of laughter and tears. Praying, praying. Praying some more.

And then—when they are grown and start to be interesting and responsible human beings you actually converse with—they leave, to live their own lives. The irony!

It happens gradually, yes, but I am realizing more and more that one of the most important parts of parenting is letting go. Not letting go of love—never that! But how necessary and loving it is for us parents to let go of the feeling that our children "owe" us. It's good for us and freeing for our children. How do you love and let go? I'm still trying to figure that out. Maybe it has something to do with being grateful for yesterday; grateful for now; grateful for who they are, now.

Gratitude frees us. It allows us to become interested observers of our grown-up children's lives, all while we pray and believe for the best for them.

My children will always have my heart, even if I don't go around reminding them of it. I agree with Solomon: *"Set me as a seal upon your heart, as a seal upon your arm; for love is as strong as death. Many waters cannot quench love, nor can the floods drown it."* It is, I think, eternal. I can't imagine that the fierce love I have for my family will die with me. As I drove away from my Montana home many years ago—first to college and then a year later with my new husband—I didn't consider what my parents were experiencing. But now, these many years later, I still know my father's approval; I still sense my mother's love; I still feel the warmth of her smile. Even now. Home doesn't leave us, even if we leave home.

> *"I thought about that old saying, how we can never go home again. But I think it's more like a piece of us stays behind when we leave—a piece we can never reclaim, one that awaits our next visit and demands that we remember."*[18]

Leaving home is a powerful stage of our development. The questions below will help you think about what it meant for you to leave home.

If you have children who are in this stage, consider what it means for you and your family for them to leave and how you can get through it gracefully and purposefully.

- What do you remember about leaving home?
- What was exciting about leaving? What was hard about it?
- Do you ever recall being homesick?
- What did you miss most about home?
- How did you get over it?
- If you have children who have left home, how has it changed them? And how has it changed you?
- How is your home different now, if you have children who have left?
- As you look back on your childhood, do you think you had a secure place from which to launch your life?
- If not, how can you offer that to yourself now?
- How can you prepare now to help your children leave?

Chapter 3

When Home Leaves You

"How do you go to your own house when something has gone bad on the inside, when it doesn't seem like your place to live anymore, when you almost cannot recall living there although it was the place you mostly ate and slept for all your grown-up life? Try to remember two or three things about living there. Try to remember cooking one meal."[19]

Some things should never happen at home. But they do.

We should not have to lose the most important person in the world to us, through death or divorce. Children should never be abandoned. Home should be a safe place for children to grow.

But sometimes we do, they are, and it isn't.

Life-controlling addictions or mental illnesses can tear a home apart. They shouldn't exist. But unfortunately, they do.

Home can heal the brokenhearted—but sometimes home breaks our hearts. Some leavings are more difficult than the kind discussed in the last chapter—made difficult by what home is, or what it isn't. It's possible to feel abandoned by your home even if you never leave it, if the adults in your home leave you, emotionally. And when you feel abandoned by your home before you are ready to leave it, you may feel lost. Or at least unsure of what to do next—of how to establish a home of your own. Addiction and abuse or illness can distress a home, leaving in its wake children and grown-ups who struggle, trying to find a solid footing. It's possible to live with dysfunction for a lifetime and until a crisis hits, we cannot see that things need to change.

When you experience a major loss of home, you can't just instantly patch everything all back together. You may have to grieve what was—or maybe what never was—to go on to establish a healthy home for yourself.

Is it possible to learn new ways of being, to have a good home when yours pretty much left you? How do you pick up the pieces and start over when the pieces weren't that great to begin with?

It is possible—by the grace of God. By seeing the truth, by getting good counsel. By making good choices.

My friend Bev shared with me her story.

Bev's story

"My childhood home was toxic. *Toxic.* That was the term my psychologist used." For Bev, what she lived was normal—not the normal that other children lived, but the normal she was accustomed to, which she always suspected was somehow off. "My home was not safe, and I knew that what went on behind our doors was not what happened at my friends' houses. I dreamed of living in that other world . . . instead I pretended to be 'normal,' and smiled and acted happy. That is how I got by. Simply put, I faked it."

Bev's mother married early in her teens and had babies right away. As Bev looks back, she realizes her mother tended to get into dysfunctional relationships, and as a consequence, home was tumultuous. Her mother, a child herself, simply did not have good coping skills.

As a little girl, Bev felt insecure, never knowing what the mood would be. Would there be angry words and fights? Would it be quiet for once, no yelling? Would she get to sleep all night, or would she be awakened and pulled from her bed as she and her mother fled for safety, terrified and in tears? Only to return the next night, usually battered and bruised.

Now, years later, Bev has been blessed with a wonderful husband and son, and through much counseling, she has been able to establish a warm, happy, and loving home. She says, "The biggest difference between my home and my mother's is God. By the grace of God, I was able to break the cycle of dysfunction that I grew up in. To say that I am eternally grateful is an understatement. You have no idea how this delights me!"

Through counseling, Bev realized for the first time that she had choices—that she could make different, good choices moving forward. She had the freedom to say no to unhealthy lifestyles, and more importantly, to say yes to healthy things. The concept of having a choice was empowering for Bev.

Bev had a good friend in high school who invited her into her home, and Bev saw modeled there what home could be. The family took Bev in as one of their own, and Bev still calls them her "parents."

"Everyone needs a house to live in, but a supportive family is what builds a home."

– Anthony Liccione

Remake your sense of home

Life happens to all of us, in one way or another. We are all given a mixed bag of experiences, and sometimes the homes we create reflect that. None of us have had perfect homes—some of us less perfect than others. Some of us have had terrible homes. But healing begins when we understand that we don't have to be victim to others' poor choices.

Proverbs 14:1 says, "The wise woman builds her house, but the foolish pulls it down with her hands." We are not victims, and how freeing it is when we realize we can choose to create the home that we need and desire.

Jason[20] showed up on our doorstep after a brief call to let us know he was coming. "Tina left me," he told us. "I don't know where else to go." When he arrived, his car was packed with clothes and a few random boxes of belongings. I couldn't believe how many shoes he had, just thrown in the back seat of his car. Bill and I shed tears with Jason, and we listened as he talked. We prayed together. Jason stayed with us for a while. The good news is that eventually Jason and Tina were able to put their home back together after counseling, forgiveness, and hard work.

But sometimes it doesn't work, no matter how hard we try to put the pieces back together. Some "broken homes" stay broken. Divorce is not ideal, but the reality is it takes two willing people to make a marriage, to work on a relationship. It's not the ideal to give up one's child for adoption, but sometimes that happens too, for complicated reasons. Desperate people do desperate things.

Our daughter Amy, whom we adopted from Korea, was left as a tiny baby on a doorstep and eventually placed in an orphanage for three years until we brought her home to us. She'd been used to sleeping on a mat on the floor, one of about 120 toddlers in the place. There was one worker for twelve children, so she was lucky to get fed and bathed. Our home must have seemed strange to her, to be surrounded by people with round, blue eyes. We persevered in trying to show love, and eventually, we bonded.

Amy's husband, Eddie, grew up with a biological family torn apart by drugs. He and his siblings were bounced from place to place in foster care for over nine years. His life changed when he was adopted into a caring and committed family. I asked Eddie how he got over it. He described the rage he often felt as an early teen—something he couldn't even articulate. He just wanted to run. "Was it anger, or was it grief?" I asked him.

"Maybe both," he said. "But I don't know that I've ever gotten over it. Ever. I just have this intense need to belong." He has learned to cope, through the love and commitment of his adoptive family (as well as much counseling), and now he and my daughter, Amy, are creating a new home together. They recently welcomed a newborn son, William Laurence, and they are committed to making a good home for each other and little Wills.

Natural disasters

Personal dynamics are not the only breakers of homes. Natural disasters and wars can wreak havoc. It is impossible to ignore current news stories of refugees who are fleeing their war-torn and famine-ravaged countries and are just trying to find some sort of refuge. At the same time, the terrifying strength of recent hurricanes Harvey and Irma devastated an untold number of homes. Enormous mudslides and earthquakes in South America have destroyed many homes and lives. Closer to my home, Oregon has had wildfires, with some homes destroyed. We wonder where on earth safe places exist, if this can happen—if we can lose our homes. But just as a physical home can be rebuilt, so can a spiritual and emotional home. It is people, after all, who make homes, and with persistence and healing, home can be restored.

> *"There is no comfort anywhere for anyone who dreads to go home."*
>
> *– Laura Ingalls Wilder*

Cultivate a Spirit of Belonging

We can be proactive in cultivating a spirit of belonging—of making the home that we long for and need. Maya Angelou wrote, "Thomas Wolfe warned . . . that 'You Can't Go Home Again.' I enjoyed the book but I never agreed with the title. I believe that one can never leave home. I believe that one carries the shadows, the dreams, the fears and dragons of home under one's skin, at the extreme corners of one's eyes and possibly in the gristle of the earlobe. Home is that youthful region where a child is the only real living inhabitant. Parents, siblings, and neighbors, are mysterious apparitions, who come, go, and do strange unfathomable things in and around the child, the region's only enfranchised citizen . . . We may act sophisticated and worldly but I believe we feel safest when we go inside ourselves and find home, a place where we belong and maybe the only place we really do."[21]

Home is a spirit of belonging that we can cultivate and protect with time. Being determined to cultivate such a home—no matter what material we have been given—is a choice that we make. Even if our home of origin was a difficult one, we can try to remember at least one positive aspect of our childhood home (and we may have to think long and hard to discover it). When we recall these positive aspects and carry them forward into our own homes in some way, we connect past to present and find where we belong in a profound way.

Bev's best memory from her childhood is of her mother baking bread. She would take a little of the dough, stretch it into a flat disc, deep-fry it, and coat it with melted butter and then the best part . . . cinnamon sugar. Bev says, "My mother called them 'dough gobs.' It was perhaps the most fabulous taste in the world. It still makes me smile to remember those wonderful days spent in the kitchen with my mom and the smell of bread baking. Now when I bake bread I make dough gobs for my son. It is a good memory I get to share with him."

Bev has made an intentional decision to make her home a place of security and unconditional love. Bev says, "Sometimes I turn down my son's bed for him at night. I start dinner early so that the house smells good when he walks in the front door. I bake brownies or cookies on the first and last day of school. There is love in the little things."

And there is healing, too, in the little things that make home uniquely ours and say, *This is our home. We belong here.* For instance, you can start your own rhythms and patterns, such as doing family chores together on Saturday morning; or having "prayer huddles" to pray together before family and friends leave; or going to church together as a family. It doesn't matter the tradition—and you can borrow freely from others—it matters that you incorporate it, and that it becomes yours.

Through care and purposeful intention, home can bring healing to ourselves and to those who dwell with us. Home can bring relief for those in pain, wholeness for the broken, and comfort for the bereft.

> *"I wanted my home to be a haven, like coming in from the cold to a big warm hug."*
>
> – *Cathy Bramley, Conditional Love*

Joseph's story

Joseph's story in Genesis is a powerful one of what it means for a young man to be forced out of his home before he is ready, and not at a time of his choosing. He was betrayed by his jealous brothers and sold into slavery in Egypt. The brothers dipped Joseph's coat in an animal's blood and showed it to their grief-stricken father as proof that he'd been killed by wild animals. Meanwhile Joseph was thrust alone into the alien world of Egypt. What a deep sense of rejection he must have felt.

But the rest of the story is that Joseph—by keeping his integrity and trusting God through the years—eventually rose to prominence in Egypt, second only to Pharaoh. Through his leadership, Egypt was able to survive years of famine, and when Joseph's brothers came to Egypt to buy grain, Joseph had an opportunity to confront them. After having a little fun at their expense, he revealed to his brothers who he was—and he forgave them. He eventually helped his father and brothers move to Egypt.[22]

Joseph's story is an amazing record of restoration. No one would have blamed Joseph if he had imprisoned his brothers when they showed up, desperate for grain. No one would have blamed Joseph for taking revenge. He had the power; he could have used it against them. But instead, he forgave his brothers, fed them, and gave them new homes in his country. He brought them in and helped them find a new country and a sense of belonging there.

Cultivate a Spirit of Forgiveness and Restoration

> *"Everyone thinks forgiveness is a wonderful idea until they have something to forgive."*[23]

Lifelong schisms in families and homes can make things hard. Reconciliation may seem impossible to attain, and it takes two to have a relationship. But we have the choice, like Joseph, to refuse to perpetuate the brokenness.

We don't have to pass it on. We can say, *"This stops here. Now."* How do we do this? Only through forgiveness; only through letting go. Genesis 39:2 says, "The Lord was with Joseph, and he was a successful man; and he was in the house of his master the Egyptian." Although Joseph lost his home in Canaan, he entered a new one in Egypt, and he thrived there.

Some of us, like Joseph, must forgive those who should have protected us and didn't. This is not easily said or done. Yet it must be—not because they deserve it, but because forgiveness is the only way to stop the dysfunction, to stop the patterns of betrayal. Some things are more difficult to forgive than others, and that is when we must let go of our expectations and trust God, the perfect judge of us all.

We may think, *He should have known better.* Or, *If he would just say he was sorry.* Or, *She needs to make restitution for this.* Or, *God could have prevented this from happening. And He didn't.* There is no debating it—life is unfair. But it is good to know that we do not have to be held hostage to old injustices, including our earliest negative experiences of home.

"Through the LORD's mercies," the prophet wrote in Lamentations 3:22, "we are not consumed." A friend who had been betrayed in the most personal of ways by both her husband and her father became aware that the only way to let go of the pain was to forgive. It was not to let them off the hook; it was not that they deserved forgiveness. But she needed to let it go for her own peace and restoration. She told me later that the best she could do at first was to take "shuffling, persistent steps" toward forgiveness, and eventually, she was restored. Her life is full and rewarding. But it did not happen instantly.

> *"Forgiveness is celestial amnesia; that is, letting go of all the memories of the past except the love we have given and received."*
>
> – *Unknown*

CULTIVATE A SPIRIT OF MAKING HEALTHY CHOICES

The first chapter of Genesis describes how our Creator made order out of chaos as he spoke our beautiful world into existence: *"And the Spirit of God was hovering over the face of the waters."*[24] What a moving scene this would have been to see: God's Spirit hovering over vast and nameless, yet-to-be productive waters, as he breathed wondrous works of creation into existence.

Since we are made in the image of God, we have that spark of creativity so that even though we may have a chaotic home life in our background, it is possible for us to catch a vision of what is possible and forge new patterns to heal our concept of home.

Home can be restored. The elephant in the room can be addressed. Help is available, and a home of grace and welcome can help heal us.

People who transcend difficult home lives often refer to someone significant in their lives who helped them do it: an aunt; a grandparent; a teacher; a mentor of some kind who simply by example, or by bringing them into their circle of belonging, helped bring healing and restoration. Someone who, like a lighthouse, showed the safe way home.

Josh Gates writes, "Home is a reflecting surface, a place to measure our growth and enrich us after being infused with the outside world."[25] How we all want to give our children that good reflecting place; that healthy launching pad that is a lifelong, life-impacting gift! The good news is, it can be done. We can all do it, no matter what lies in the past.

> *"It is a great deal better to live a holy life than to talk about it. Lighthouses do not ring bells and fire cannons to call attention to their shining. They just shine!"*
>
> *– D.L. Moody*

Don't wait; start where you are

We may have to take matters into our own hands to create the childhood home we never had. John Argue writes poignantly about the chronic homesickness he felt as an orphan, even after he was grown. He realized he had been waiting for the right woman who would help him make a home. That didn't seem to be happening, so he decided to make a home for himself. He says, "I bought my first cookbook, dishes, matching towels, a bed, a bookcase. Now, fourteen years later, my bread-and-butter pickles are famous, cut flowers from my garden grace my desk and mantelpiece, and my fig-ginger jam is legendary . . . Our weary, alienated nation suffers from nearly universal homesickness; we are a nation of orphans. Many believe that we cannot have a home without a partner or a mortgage. Against this some of us have chosen to affirm that right where we are is enough. Home-making remains the true, perennial center of the only civilized life that really matters."[26]

> *"Are we running away from home?" I asked, giving voice to the question that had been on my mind for two days, ever since the lady at the Wok On restaurant asked where we were from and my mother lied.*
>
> *My mother had laughed. I couldn't see her face, but her laugh I could always conjure – rich, ringing, like bells calling you to a wedding. "No, silly goose. You can't run away from home. It's not home if you want to run away from it." She paused to brush a strand of hair from my face. "You can only run away from a house. Home is something you run toward."*[27]

Remake your sense of home

Perhaps you feel that instead of leaving home as a young person, your home left *you.* You may be struggling now with how to find and make the home that you want and need. Reflect on the three concepts listed below to see how you can incorporate them now.

- **Cultivate a Sense of Belonging:** ***What examples of belonging have I seen in other homes and families? How can I encourage that in myself and my own future home?***
- **Cultivate a Spirit of Forgiveness:** ***Do I have any unfinished business or wounds from my past home that may be dictating some unhealthy patterns today? I choose to make it a priority to write down any offenses that come to mind and prayerfully let them go into God's good and just hands.***
- **Cultivate the Habit of Making Healthy Choices:** ***What are some life-affirming choices I can begin to make that will help make my present and future home (and my own self) healthy?***

Chapter 4

Coming Home

"We search for a self to be. We search for other selves to love. We search for work to do. And since even when to one degree or another we find these things, we find also that there is still something crucial missing which we have not found; we search for that unfound thing too, even though we do not know its name or where it is to be found or even if it is to be found at all."[28]

– Frederick Buechner

When do you stop looking for your own place? When do you know deep inside that where you are is finally home? *Your* home. Restless souls that we are, we all seek a place of refuge out of which to live our lives. We wonder, *Where shall we live? How do we make that place home?*

As I write today, I am sitting at a gate in an airport terminal. My flight has been delayed, and I am being rebooked (hopefully). Like many people here, I just want to get home. There are delays due to weather, and I can't help but notice the stress on people's faces as they run through the tarmac, trying to catch their connecting flight. You can spot the road warriors, the ones with the frequent miles, determined to get back for that baseball game or that ballet recital.

We all want to get home, wherever it is—even if it's just to our comfy bed or our neurotic cat.

Home is where we can relax; a place out of which we can live our lives. But early in our lives, home can seem as temporary and as transient as we are. As we try to figure out our work, our relationships, and our goals, home for a time stays by the wayside.

Temporary homes, temporary places

> *"It is a great comfort to a rambling people to know that somewhere there is a permanent home – perhaps it is the most final of the comforts they ever really know."*[29]

My early homes were temporary: Montana, growing up. Southern California in the sixties, an adventure. Early marriage took me many new places, and I tried to make homes along the way, yet I never really put down roots in those early places.

If we want to be real about it, most of our homes are temporary. It takes intention to give yourself to a place—to invest in it emotionally and physically, to make it yours. I have thought at times, "I don't want to get involved with my neighbors or this community because I may move again. I don't want to put too much into this house (or this apartment) because I'm not sure how long I'll be here."

My grandmother Maud never owned a home, but she moved from place to place as a widow during the Depression, staying wherever she could, sometimes renting a room in a house. My mother told me, however, that no matter where they lived, Grandma somehow made the place home. She cleaned it until it shone, put down rugs she'd made, and always managed to put on a tasty, warm supper when the day ended, even if it was cooked over a single burner in a bedroom. She had a fierce drive to create a place of privacy and protection from a sometimes hostile and untrustworthy world.

When I was small, I could never understand what I thought to be a very inhospitable attitude on my grandmother's part toward my friends and neighbors. She didn't want visitors other than her own family, and she let us know that right up front. Now that I reflect on her situation, I realize she was used to fighting for a home for herself and her children, and she was often at the mercy of others to provide that place, no matter how temporary it was. When she had a place that was truly hers, she guarded it.

I didn't fully appreciate home until after I left it, and then it took a few years of school and early marriage for me to realize that home was where I was—not where my parents, my siblings, or my farm was. My new husband and I returned as often as we could to my parents' place in Montana, but it was to visit, not to stay. Going home was not the same. Leaving had changed me, changed home for me.

Homemaking is experimental at first, like a waystation on our way to something better. If it's available to us, maybe we bounce back to our childhood home often when we're first getting established. Then we finally get our own apartment, or a condo that we share with roommates. We experiment with preparing food, surprised by the constant challenge of having to buy ingredients and prepare something edible—usually within a limited budget. I remember discovering frozen chicken pot pies for under a dollar. What a wonderful invention, I thought. Forty minutes in the oven, and *voila!*

After we left San Francisco, Bill and I stayed in the downstairs apartment of his parents' house for a few months while we were both working, and Bill was going to graduate school. Then we housesat for a family for a few months until we got our own apartment. Moving was not that hard, as all we had was a bed and a dresser and our clothes. And a lot of tablecloths.

In San Francisco, for the first time in my life, I encountered homeless people.

Homeless! Even the word brings a desolate feeling. I am painfully aware as I write this of a recent statistic that says close to 600,000 adults are homeless in America.[30] That doesn't even count teenagers and young people.

The solutions are not simple, but there are good people working hard to help, and we can get involved too, even in small ways.[31] Mental illness and addiction are often factors among the homeless. It's also true that some people simply fall on hard times, get priced out of the housing market, and find themselves without a place they can call home.

Homelessness reminds us of how precious and tenuous home is; how we must search for it, and when we find it, protect it and care for it the best we can.

> *"It might be well enough to wander if you've a place and people to come back to, but I tell you now there's no desolation like wanting to go home and truly not knowing where it is."*
>
> *– Elizabeth Kerner*

THE POSSIBILITY OF A BETTER PLACE

> *"Give me your tired, your poor, your huddled masses yearning to breathe free, The wretched refuse of your teeming shore. Send these, the homeless, tempest-tost to me: I lift my lamp beside the golden door."*
>
> *– Emma Lazarus, inscription on the Statue of Liberty*

People on a search for home is nothing new. Moses led the Israelites out of Egypt toward their promised land in an epic, forty-year-long saga. Jesus lamented that even though the sparrow had a nest, he didn't have a home, and then he reminded us of the dwelling places he was preparing for us.

Our country was built by immigrants, my ancestors among them. Even now, multitudes of people are looking for homes, desperately wanting a place to call their own. When Bill and I visited Turkey and Malta this past year, we became aware of the many refugees fleeing their homes, forced out by war and famine, searching for a safe place for themselves and their families. Many in the world are risking their lives to find a place called home.

Home is an ever-evolving, ever-growing concept. We need a place for wherever we are in life. And home is as individual as we are.

What keeps us from putting down roots? Maybe it's holding onto an ideal of what home should look like as we wait for something better—fair enough, I suppose, but that may be allowing the future to rob us of the present. We can make our temporary place home now.

Here's what we must understand about finding home: *we* make our place home, and finding our home starts where we are now.

"I want your life," sixteen-year-old Brianna told me. She was having trouble navigating adolescence, so through a program in our church, I agreed to be her mentor. I gave her some odd jobs to do around our house, as she wanted to earn extra money. We were spreading bark dust in the backyard when she told me what she really wanted was to have a life and a house just like mine. "Oh, Brianna, you have no idea what it takes to maintain my life," I laughed.

My friend Dawn moves at least once a year. It's become almost humorous, as every time I see her, she tells me she is moving because she hates where she lives. It's a neighbor with a barking dog; or she doesn't like the appliances in the kitchen; or she can't get the air-conditioning to work right; or there's a toxic smell in the new carpet that she just can't stand. There's no question that some places are difficult. There are times to move. But nothing is perfect, not even the most fabulous home.

Meghan Daum writes, "For so long, maybe all my life, I thought only a house could make you whole. I thought I was nothing without an interesting address. I thought I was only as good as my color scheme, my drawer pulls, my floors . . . it's the knowledge that a house can be as fragile as life itself. You'd think it would be stronger, since it can stand in one spot for centuries while generations of humans run through its rooms, grow up, move out, and eventually die. But a house is an inherently limited entity. It can't do everything, or even most things. It cannot give you a personality. It cannot bring you love. It cannot cure loneliness. It can provide comfort, safety, a sense of pride—that much I know."[32]

It's a beautiful thing to dream of the place we can have, if it inspires us where we are or galvanizes us to something better. Whole industries are built on the concept of fixing up homes, making them more beautiful and livable. But we can waste a lot of energy longing for something we don't have or can't afford. It's tempting to compare our place with others' places. We may have a one-bedroom, but our neighbor has a two-bedroom-two-bath apartment . . . with a patio, or even a garage. A friend or a relative may live in a gated community while we live in a small condo downtown, and we wish we had her community pool and paved bike paths. Or we drive through a neighborhood of custom-built homes and wonder what it would be like to live there. Surely, that would be complete happiness and contentment! If only we had *that* house! With that yard and that view. We visit model homes and think, *If I had a house like this, my life would be perfect!*

But envy is deceptive. It blinds us from seeing what we do have, and then we can't connect emotionally with where we are. We haven't "moved in" yet, as we're still waiting for something else.

Our homes reflect who we are. It takes a great deal of understanding and investment of ourselves to make any home the good place that it can be—no matter the address or the size. The wise king who owned a most beautiful home wrote, "Through wisdom a house is built; and by understanding it is established; by knowledge the rooms are filled with all precious and pleasant riches."[33] It takes time—maybe years—to create home.

> *"The heartland lies where the heart longs to be. Sometimes it takes a lifetime to find the true place to plant it."*[34]

Home requires something of us

> *"A man builds a fine house; and now he has a master, and a task for life is to furnish, watch, show it, and keep it in repair the rest of his life."*[35]

Can we afford our home? Thoreau wrote, "The price of anything is the amount of life you exchange for it." Bigger is not necessarily better, if it's a financial strain. Where we live is not only a financial obligation, but it requires a certain amount of energy and maintenance. Location is important too; no matter how perfect the home is in price, if it's too far from where your people are, or your work is, it may not be the place for you. And the price is not only financial, but also time and energy. What do you want to mortgage your life for? Is it worth it?

Go ahead and search. But likewise, be content. It may seem a paradox, but as Scripture says, "contentment is great gain."[36]

Comparing our place to others' places is like comparing ourselves with others. We look at another person's life—their profession, their work or family—and envy them. We wish we had what they had. Famous, well-off people may seem to have the ideal home and life. But we have no concept of the mental, physical, and financial cost required to live that life. Never envy the one who seems to have a better home, a better life than you. Envy is wasted energy, as we have no true concept of what it takes to maintain that home, that life. Be inspired by others, but not envious.

After Bill finished his graduate degree and our first son, Jon, was born, we moved from our diverse and dynamic church in San Francisco and our many friends to a small rental near the beach in Aptos, California. I adored my baby son, but we only had one car, so when Bill went to his teaching job, I felt lonely and isolated. The house next door to ours was bigger (huge, it seemed to me), and the family there had two small children and a lot of friends and family who came and went.

Their life made my loneliness more acute. I wanted what my neighbor had: a bigger house, and lots of people coming and going. In the home of my childhood, I was surrounded with chaos and people. Laughter and preparing food and constant talk; these things were my comfort zone. I eventually realized that it was up to me to create the home I wanted, so I began to reach out to others, made new friends, and invited people over. And I started to feel at home in that place. My brother Dan came to live with us for a while, and other family members would come to visit. I realize now that what finally made it home to me was having people *in*.

What I didn't know then—and I have a lot of compassion for the young woman who was me—is that an understanding and acceptance of oneself is essential to building a good, strong life and a good, strong home. It took me many years to understand and value myself. *"Know thyself, and to thine own self be true,"*[37] Shakespeare wrote.

> *"Daughter am I in my mother's house; But mistress in my own."*[38]

We interact with our homes

As we live in our childhood homes, we bring soul and life and creativity into them. But when we leave our childhood home—perhaps marry—we begin to make our own lives and searching for home is an individual search.

While my comfort zone meant being surrounded by people, as a child I also spent a lot of time outside, reading and thinking, writing in my journal. So, while I love being around people, I also crave solitude—I need space after being with people for a while. Within your home, it is important to create places that nourish your own soul, as well as places that nourish others who come there. We must take responsibility for our own needs.

But even when we do get settled in a place, often there remains in the back of our minds a nagging sense that maybe there's another place out there, a better place to make our own. And since it may be true that home is people, we search for our people. Perhaps a spouse. Then we look for a place to contain our lives.

> *"I have come back again to where I belong; not an enchanted place, but the walls are strong."*[39]

Describe your first home or two away from home. Maybe you are there now, in what feels like a waystation. How can you make it into the home you are looking for?

- How did you furnish your first "grown-up" home?
- What made it good?
- What was the first place that felt like home to you?
- What was your comfort zone in your childhood home, and how has that affected what kind of home you long for and need now?
- Is there an ideal home that you have in mind? Describe it.

CHAPTER 5

Yes Where You Are

"For just one second, look at your life and see how perfect it is. Stop looking for the next secret door that is going to lead you to your real life. Stop waiting. This is it: there's nothing else. It's here, and you'd better decide to enjoy it or you're going to be miserable wherever you go."[40]

It was our first house—small, but perfect for our growing family. At least it seemed perfect to us. We had found a lot to build on that had some challenges, but with Bill's creativity and his father's building expertise, we built our home, perched on a hillside over Aptos Valley in California. We loved every inch of it, and we did much of the work to get it built. Our furnishings were sparse, but the house's best feature made up for it: a large wraparound deck with an expansive view of the apple orchard in the valley below. The house was drenched in sunshine, surrounded by vivid splashes of orange and yellow wild California poppies. We were ecstatic to have a place of our own to host family and friends. It was secluded and peaceful. As I said—perfect.

We had only lived there for a year and a half when Bill received a call from a church in Albany, Oregon. Would we consider moving there to join a growing church? After taking a visit to Oregon, Bill was excited about the challenge of being involved in ministry. Our lives at that point were secure: Bill had a position in a school district that offered growth. We were expecting our second son. But Bill wasn't ready for security; he wanted challenge and the opportunity to be involved in a growing church. With mixed emotions, I agreed.

We sold the beautiful home of our dreams and moved to Albany, Oregon, an industrial town nestled in the Willamette Valley. We moved into a small duplex crammed amongst many others just like them until we could find a bigger place. We literally could see what our neighbors were having for breakfast, as there were no privacy screens.

Ten days after we moved, Eric was born, and we became parents of two. I loved my baby boys, but I missed my view. I missed my privacy. Is it possible to grieve for a house? Of course. Our first new house had been small, but it was beautiful, and I grieved the loss of it.

We were now in a different place in life—on staff with a large church, where my life was not my own and Bill was swamped with his new duties. I had no time for contemplation or privacy, not to mention trying to meet the demands of a two-year-old, a new baby, and a too-busy husband. I hadn't really met anyone yet, and I was unsure what was required of me. I was desperately unhappy. Something had to change.

One Sunday in the back row of the church, as I tried to keep my babies content, I shot up a one-word prayer to God: *Yes.*

I felt inadequate for where I was. I didn't know what was ahead of me. But I sensed I had a choice: say *Yes;* or keep wanting something else, something better, something I used to have instead of what I had now.

There's something powerful about saying Yes where we are. If you're like me, sometimes you look at the place where you are and say, "This is not what I wanted." We long for something different, or for a place that we once had.

Looking back, saying *Yes* didn't change the place, but it changed me in the place. I grew to love it there.

> *"The entire time I've been thinking about where my home was. At first it was California, then Wisconsin. But in truth, home isn't necessarily where you sleep at night. It's where you feel like yourself. Where you're most comfortable. Where you don't have to pretend, where you can just be you."*[41]

LOVE WHERE YOU LIVE

> *"The best rooms also have something to say about the people who live in them."*
>
> – *David Hicks*

Maybe you've had this experience: You walk into your house and exclaim, *"What a dump!"* You may hate where you live right now. I have been there, so I understand. It can take a conscious choice to embrace where we are.

Try to understand your emotions about your house right now, especially if they are negative. It's an awful feeling to feel that you are stuck. If you are limited by what you can afford and what is available to you—and often this is the case—it's important to accept that this is just where you are for now. Look at how you think about your home and ask yourself seriously how you can begin to embrace where you are.

Maybe your house is just messy, or you do not feel you are in a safe or good neighborhood. If that's the case, reach out to meet your neighbors. It may help to find a friendly face or two. And it's possible that rearranging furniture or getting rid of something can open some space and light in your house and make it feel more like your place.

Every place has its drawbacks and limitations, and we either learn to live with them, or we learn to see them in a new light and make whatever changes we can. If you are renting a home, you may view that as a drawback. Instead, it can be liberating: the owner of the house must deal with its maintenance; you can make the home livable for you. Many landlords appreciate renters who want to improve their place, and yours may give you a reduction on your rent if you negotiate painting a room or get new flooring.

Loving where you live may take some time. Truthfully, this is an ongoing process, because where we live will change (more so for some of us than for others). If you are living in a place you love, good for you. But there are times we all struggle to like where we live.

Saying Yes where you are takes work and flexibility; it's an ongoing process of making a home wherever we are. My friend LaJuana grew up as a child of itinerant evangelists who traveled the United States and Canada. She remembers home as being in a car—with her parents and her little brother—on the road, pulling a small trailer that held all their musical instruments. LaJuana's parents were called to that life and embraced it wholeheartedly. The open road was their home.

Unlike LaJuana, I was not used to an itinerant life. I was used to staying in one house, one community. But as a young couple, Bill and I moved a lot, depending on Bill's work. Pastoral ministry called for flexibility in many areas. After our duplex experience, we moved to a new house in North Albany where we added our third son to our family. We were now parents of three little boys: Jon, Eric, and Chris. Life was so busy, and things changed so fast, that I didn't realize what powerfully important years they were when I was a young mom, trying to figure it all out, loving and caring for my babies, supporting my husband, and somehow trying to keep a sense of self.

Our fourth son, Andy, was born in Salem, Oregon, where we began to become involved in publishing and writing. We made a big step when we decided we would move to central Oregon, where we started our own publishing company. We built a house at Black Butte Ranch and a few years later, adopted our daughter, Amy. I loved the house at Black Butte deeply, and I truly made it mine. Maybe that house meant so much to me—to all of us—because we lived there for twenty-two years. It was the most formative place of our children's lives as well as our professional lives. Still, no place is perfect, and if I am honest, I can remember the imperfections of it too. The living room was too small. It was too far from our school and church and town. But we loved it. It was home.

And of course, as I shared at the beginning of this book, we left it too.

Places where we live are just stopping places on the journey that makes up the whole picture of our life. What makes these places powerful and lasting are the people we get to know and love in them.

Back when I was a young wife and mother, it seemed my whole life was ahead of me—a journey that would take me someplace wonderful. That sense of vision brought restlessness with it. There would always a better place, a better situation. Deep within me was a continual sense of looking for adventure and discovery amid marriage, five children, writing, and ministry. And not just seeking the place; it was the sense of wanting to be more, do more. Live more.

But I have seen that in striving for a better place, we often miss the wonderfulness of our ordinary spot, just where we are. Saying Yes where we are is at times, difficult. The wait for what makes the Yes good can take years. It can take perspective. Author Elisabeth Elliot suffered many losses and setbacks in her life. She persevered in saying Yes through the deaths of two husbands. Her words show the weight of tested truth: "Some of God's greatest mercies are in his refusals. He says no in order that he may, in some way we cannot imagine, say yes."

Brother Lawrence was a monk in the 1600s who worked in the kitchen and decided he could do his common, ordinary chores all for the love of God. As he worked in the yard, he mused that he could even pick up a piece of straw for the love of God.[42]

Common, ordinary chores can become extraordinary, and we can practice the presence of God even in the ordinary moments and the imperfect places. I have found that it certainly does take practice. Practice being thankful for the energy to do ordinary chores, thankful for the beauty in the present moment. We tend to be driven by the urgent, and we miss the being where we are.

It is true; ordinary can be quite maddening. It's so unremarkable. So boring. But if I look closer, I see that the ordinary moments reveal our motives (something Jesus talked about a lot). Ordinary moments reveal who we are.

The truth is that it's the ordinary that is so special. Ask a refugee: *Wouldn't an ordinary home-cooked meal in the family home with those you love be wonderful?* Ask someone who has lost a spouse: *Wouldn't an ordinary day of doing chores or riding bikes together be extraordinary?* Ask someone who is desperately ill: *How would you like an ordinary day, free from pain?*

When I managed to say *Yes* to my little duplex in a cramped neighborhood, somehow it became transformed into a place of productivity, of hospitality. It slowly became home. Jesus said, "Blessed are the meek"—and another meaning for that is "content." Blessed are the content, for they shall inherit the earth. Which is exactly what the discontent, the ambitious want to do. What I want to do. Inherit the earth. Succeed.

Home is a fixed place, at the very core of who we are. And we *make* home as we surround and fill our places with ourselves.

> *"What was home, really? Just a place to lay your head.*
>
> *No. It was so much more than that. It was a place where a person belonged. Where a fellow would*

be missed. It was a part of a man. Something that couldn't be sold or taken for granted."[43]

To find your home is to be found

"It may be argued that the past is a country from which we have all emigrated, that its loss is part of our common humanity."[44]

We are all refugees needing safe places along the way. The psalmist wrote about his heart being "set on pilgrimage."[45] We are all on a journey, and our dwelling places change for a variety of reasons. Home is our most basic desire, and we all long for that actual, physical place of refuge; a place of restoration and a place out of which to grow and learn and give.

Homesickness brings an ache and a longing, and there is no remedy for it other than being with loved ones, being in a place where you are known and loved.

I remember being fiercely homesick a few years ago when we were staying in an industrial city. We were there on business, and I knew it was a temporary stay, but I remember trying in vain to sleep, counting the minutes, the days when I would be home again. Home to my place. Where I could open the window wide at night to hear the wind sighing through the pine trees and hear the coyotes howl. Home, where I could hear the birdsong at first light, not sirens and traffic.

Our homes change over the years. Still, I must admit that much of the time I still struggle with being where I am. So now again, I choose to say *Yes* in this place, because I have learned that God always starts with where we are, with what we have.

Here's what I've seen: A place can start to shape you. We use the material that we have been given in the past to furnish the place we are now . . . but God works with us where we are. We look back with gratitude; we let go. We savor and embrace the present.

Elisha asked the desperate widow, "What do you have in your house?" And her response was like ours so often: "Nothing. Oh . . . except a jar of oil."[46] Opportunity is right before you, if you will only see it. Holy ground is right beneath your feet. Maybe the very best place—even if it feels temporary—is where you are, now. In your own place—whatever it is.

Home is a strong metaphor for our own selves, and I believe that until we are truly at home with who we are, we continuously struggle to be at home in any place. Samuel Butler wrote, "Every man's work, whether it be literature or music or pictures or architecture or anything else, is always a portrait of himself."[47]

To come home means to grow up. It's not all about you—and yet it is. Richard Rohr writes, "When you get your 'Who am I' questions asked, all the 'What shall I do' questions tend to take care of themselves."[48] Coming home helps us answer who we are, and then we can make a home, live a home, with integrity and power. We are standing on the shoulders of many who have shown us the way. We are their heirs; we have an inheritance. And with it, we build our own homes.

Don't wait for that perfect place. It doesn't exist.

> *"It isn't what you have or who you are or where you are or what you are doing that makes you happy or unhappy. It's what you think about it."*[49]

No matter what circumstances you find yourself in, you can make that place home. Admittedly, some places take more imagination and intention. Maybe the home you are looking for is where you are. Maybe the best work for you is in the talents and gifts and relationships you have now.

Take a clear-eyed look to see what's in front of you. Go ahead and search but say *Yes* where you are. The Yes will lead you home.

Come home, gypsy soul. Come home to yourself.

> *"Home is the place you return to when you have finally lost your soul. Home is the place where life is born, not the place of your birth, but the place where you seek rebirth. When you no longer have to remember which tale of your own past is true and which is an invention, when you know that you are an invention, then is the time to seek out your home. Perhaps only when you have come to understand that can you finally reach home."*
>
> *– Karen Maitland, Company of Liars*

As you look at the place where you are now, what emotions do you have regarding it? Are they negative or positive? If you are discussing this in a small group, discuss a home where you once lived (or where you now live) that you wanted to leave.

- What potential lies in the place where you are now?
- How can you respond to that potential?
- Are you content where you are? Or do you want something else? Do you think this is a good or a bad thing?
- What investment of time, money and inconvenience are you willing to spend to live where you want to live? Do you think it would be worth it?
- God always starts where we are. See the place right in front of you: "The ground before you is holy. Take off your shoes."

Chapter 6

Home Work

. . . housekeeping actually offers more opportunities for savoring achievement than almost any other work I can think of. Each of its regular routines brings satisfaction when it is completed. These routines echo the rhythm of life, and the housekeeping rhythm is the rhythm of the body.

You get satisfaction not only from the sense of order, cleanliness, freshness, peace and plenty restored, but from the knowledge that you yourself and those you care about are going to enjoy these benefits.[50]

Let's face it: In all the lovely thoughts of home we can forget what makes it happen: *Housework.*

A whole book could be written on how to keep your house clean. In fact, hundreds have—and I have three of those books on my shelf right now. One of them just inspired me to take another pass at my closet and fill a box with things that didn't spark joy. One woman said,

"I tried that Japanese decluttering trend where you hold each thing you own and throw it out if it doesn't give you joy. So far I've thrown out all the vegetables and the electric bill." Okay, there are a lot of things in my house that don't spark joy, but I'm working at it. It's not easy to care for a home while writing a book. Or while working at a job or raising children.

If you can hire someone to clean, good for you, but having someone do the cleaning doesn't let you off the hook. There's maintenance and care and stewardship that goes into running a home. And there's a lot of creative puttering that goes into making a house a home.

A house can be a taskmaster (as tasks may never end), and yet with a little organization and planning, it's possible to keep an attractive, welcoming home no matter what its appraised value is or if you rent or own. Let's face it—how we care for our home and the things in it is a matter of stewardship as well as a response of gratitude to God for what we have—and it signals a willingness to use these things for good. *Housework* also calls for balance. It's possible to become consumed by having everything perfect and miss having a home of peace and comfort where you can celebrate the best things in life.

My grandmother Maud knew how to keep a home, even though she never actually owned one. I remember coming to her small studio apartment on Saturdays. My dad would drop me and my sister Judy off at Grandma's apartment, and after she fed us vegetable soup, we would walk across town for our piano lessons at Mrs. Bain's. Upon entering Grandma's tiny apartment, we felt welcomed by a tangible sense of peace and order.

There was a place for everything, and everything was in its place.

Grandma's apartment contained a small table in the ell of her kitchen; a bed with a pink satin coverlet; and a big, overstuffed chair with a lamp next to it on an end table that held her Bible, usually open. A basket of her knitting was on the floor next to the chair. Grandma had a hard life, but as she grew older, she became an avid reader of the Bible, and I think she received healing from it.

When pears were in season, Grandma would make jars of her pear conserve and put them in her window to cool. Their jeweled tones of pears, cherries, and pineapples were like stained-glass windows. Eating her pear conserve spread on toast or on an English muffin was like experiencing nirvana.[51] Although I have her recipe and have tried to make it, it's never as good as Grandma's. I'm sure there's some secret ingredient I'm missing!

I have come to believe that how we care for our homes reflects how we see ourselves. I am grateful that my grandmother experienced peace and comfort in her later years, and her tiny home reflected it. The opposite can also be true. In our early lives, we can experience shame and disappointment. As a result, we give up, we let things go. We don't reach out. And our homes reflect that and don't nourish us as they could. No matter our experience, we can grow.

The cleansing power of home

When I was in college, I took a part-time job as a nanny for a single parent who was ill. She was an older woman who had been a college professor but now spent most of her days in a pullout bed in her small studio apartment in a cheap motel. I don't know if she was sick or depressed or both, but somehow her life had taken a turn, and she was estranged from her grown children as well as the father of her toddler. It was unclear how she came to be there; all I knew was that she was alone with a three-year-old son. Her little place was filthy and neglected, and I scraped years of grease off the old gas stove, scrubbed the countertops and the floors, and vacuumed the worn carpet.

I still remember the stale cigarette smell of the little hole in the wall that was her home. Her food situation was sketchy, so I bought groceries and helped her prepare meals. Three times a week after my classes, I went over to her place to clean and took time to play with the little boy on a patch of lawn in front of the motel. But I was busy with my own life and finally told her that I couldn't continue, although she begged me to stay on. What I remember most about working for her is the satisfaction I felt in making a home in a bad place. She needed help, and I was willing to give it. Maybe I was also trying to make a home for myself, a homesick college freshman.

There is a creative aspect to making a home wherever you are, even if you're not in the place you eventually want to be. A clean, safe home, with a meal simmering. Simple—yet that is the essence of home.

> *"I always wondered why the makers leave housekeeping and cooking out of their tales. Isn't it what all the great wars and battles are fought for—so that at day's end a family may eat together in a peaceful house?"*[52]

The Power of Little Things

> *"Home is not where you have to go but where you want to go; nor is it a place where you are sullenly admitted, but rather where you are welcomed – by the people, the walls, the tiles on the floor, the flowers beside the door, the play of life, the very grass."*
>
> *– Scott Russell Sanders*

A clean guest bathroom, with clean guest towels. A coaster on the coffee table on which we can put our drink. It is the little things that invite others in, help them relax, make them feel as if you prepared a welcome for them. The little things help those of us who live there too.

One sunny day not long ago I realized our house was showing the effects of two years of book deadlines and speaking, not to mention twenty years of bringing more stuff *in* than we took *out*. I had managed to keep a semblance of order, but my house was fast approaching critical mass—the clutter now overflowing onto counters and things bulging out of drawers. It was time to stop and do some deep cleaning.

I knew this would be no simple task, so I went room by room, starting in the attic—doing a little each day, one drawer, one closet. My cleaning project often got derailed as I found things to linger over. A romantic card from Bill, snapshots of friends and family. A letter from Chris shortly after he went away to college, thanking me for teaching him "the important things." (It made me cry.) I uncovered a report Andy did in high school in which he wrote, *"Our big old soft-hearted house has more memories than New York City has people,"* and he went on to write about them, and I found myself laughing. I found a dresser filled with sports clippings from newspapers when Jon and Eric were in high school (what high hopes we all had for basketball!). Prom pictures; concert programs; awards. Amy loved to draw, and I found many sketches that she did. These things go in the category of "Precious Clutter." I threw away some; I boxed the rest and gave it to my children for them to keep or throw away. For things pertaining to my grandchildren, I purchased small plastic containers, and I labeled them individually for each set of grandchildren to store school pictures and other treasures that remind me of them.

G.K. Chesterton wrote: "There are two ways to get enough. One is to accumulate more and more. The other is to desire less." "Enough" is a word I am trying to embrace.

When we do the work of caring for our homes, we discover a humility and deep connection to who we are. We deal with our excesses; we repent of them. We take responsibility for our messes. We rejoice in our past, our present, and our future as we dust pictures of our parents and things that mean something to us. We prepare our home to function as best as it possibly can to minister to our own needs as well as to others.

The passion for home runs deep. And while home is a spiritual, powerful place, it is also a physical place that takes work and stewardship. The work of home makes it ours.

Augustine wrote centuries ago,

> *"O Lord, the house of my soul is narrow; enlarge it that you may enter in. It is ruined.*
>
> *O repair it! It displeases your sight; I confess it, I know.*

But who shall cleanse it, or to whom shall I cry but you?
Cleanse me from secret faults, O Lord, and spare your servant from strange sins."[53]

Entering your home

"I would like to travel light on this journey of life, to get rid of the encumbrances I acquire each day. Worse than physical acquisitions are spiritual ones . . . I don't understand how and why I come to be only as I lose myself, but I know from long experience that this is so."

– Madeleine L'Engle

A study by the American Cleaning Institute says eliminating excess clutter reduces the amount of housework in the average home by 40 percent[54]. As you walk in your front door, what emotion do you feel when you first enter? Is there room to breathe, to see? Does it seem to be a welcoming place? How does your home smell? That cabbage soup you had last night may be nourishing, but today, the odor lingers. You may need to open a few windows or light a candle.

Does it seem clean? Are the surfaces of the counters relatively cleared of clutter? Floors swept, vacuumed, things picked up? I confess I can be messy, but I have learned the importance of having a place for things and then simply putting them in that place—perhaps the best defense against clutter.

I'm sure my childhood home had clutter, with seven children and my mother's many hobbies and crafts, but I don't remember the clutter bothering me. Maybe because it wasn't *my* clutter. Dealing with clutter is my biggest challenge. Often, when I make a list of things to do for the house, I simply write on my list, "Clutter." I know what that means: get rid of junk mail; put things back where they belong; toss what needs to be tossed. I know what to do; the challenge is in the simple discipline to develop that ongoing habit. When we put it off, clutter becomes a bigger job and takes more effort.

The priority of dealing with mail and email is a continuing challenge for me, because it represents something I need to do that I haven't done. A graduation notice I need to respond to. An unpaid bill. Thank-you notes that need to be written. A lovely card and picture of a reader's family who have read *"Lord, Bless My Child,"*[55] which I fully intend to answer.

Clutter can distract us from living our best life. Marie Kondo,[56] a Japanese organizing consultant, has written a simple yet groundbreaking book that has changed the living habits of many. She suggests that you put your hands on everything you own and ask yourself if it sparks joy. If it doesn't, thank it for its service and get rid of it. Then, she says, when only your joy-giving belongings remain, put every item in a place where it's visible, accessible, and easy to reach and then put back. Kondo's refreshing approach has inspired me to analyze my buying habits, to be more conscious of what I buy (or don't buy). I repent of buying clothes that were a fabulous deal but are not flattering, and which I have no intention of wearing. It's a waste of money.

When we refuse to bring excess things into our houses, we allow breathing room into our homes—which, in turn, helps us live a less consumer-oriented lifestyle. One study found that women who left cereal sitting on their kitchen counters weighed an average of twenty pounds more than those who had empty counters. Those who didn't put away soda weighed about twenty-six pounds more.[57] This is a pretty compelling argument for clearing clutter from the kitchen counter. I have learned that if I put cookies in the freezer, they don't get eaten as fast. Out of sight, out of mind.

Peter Walsh, author of *Lose the Clutter, Lose the Weight,* recruited a test panel of twenty-five participants who had both weight and clutter issues. Each was put through a six-week decluttering program. He says, "The results were pretty astounding. Every test panelist lost an average of ten pounds. And they all declared their homes were far more organized than when they had begun."[58]

But maybe the more important thing to do is to look a little deeper: Why do I have so much clutter? Lisa Avellan of *Simple & Soul* says: "Minimalism isn't about your stuff; it's about your soul—the 'you' underneath all of the stuff." It's more about making decisions about what we need instead of getting what we want.

> *"Better a handful with quietness Than both hands full, together with toil and grasping for the wind."*
>
> *–Ecclesiastes 4:6, NKJV*

Ten Principles to Clear Clutter[59]

1. Stop the flow of stuff coming in.
2. Declutter at least one item a day.
3. Declutter the easy stuff first.
4. Put a disposal plan in place.

5. Decide not to keep things out of guilt or obligation.
6. Do not be afraid to let go.
7. Remember that gifts do not have to be material.
8. Do not over-equip your home.
9. Do not declutter things that are not yours without the owner's permission.
10. Do not waste your life on clutter.

Digital clutter

Added to our overflowing closets is the reality that our iPhones are overflowing with information and constant intrusion. My iPhone can do miraculous things. It gives me directions; I can shop with it; I can let my people know when I will be home. I can see brand-new pictures of my second cousin's grandchild. We get *breaking news* that lets us know who's winning the U.S. Open. Or that someone in our Twitter verse likes someone's else's tweet. Urgent bits of information that we must know.

I was stopped at a red light, and ahead of me was a young mom with two children in the back seat. With one hand she was texting on a device near the steering wheel; with her other hand, she reached over to give one of her kids a sippy cup. All while waiting for the light to change to green. I admit that if I'd had an iPhone when my children were small, I'd probably have done the same thing.

Digital clutter can add to our sense of overload, and some psychological studies indicate that it is having a negative impact on us. Life is to be lived in the real world, not the virtual one. The Internet is like coffee—when used in moderation, there are health benefits. When it becomes addictive or is used too much, it can have negative effects, and it can create more sedentary behavior and social isolation.

But the Internet, of course, is here to stay. Instead of seeing it as a barrier, we can use it to help us communicate as well as get information. My twelve-year-old grandson Jackson showed me how to get more out of my phone using "Tips." To communicate with Will, my college sophomore, I text him and usually hear right back. Hudson, our seven-year-old grandson in California, likes to "FaceTime" us, usually around 4:30 in the afternoon. I can generally reach our teenaged granddaughters Kendsy and Cali by using Instagram. Hogan and Wesley also use Instagram, and Pearson and Annabelle actually like to talk to me on the phone from time to time. Technology helps us connect. With my siblings and friends, we often use private messaging through Facebook. I adore seeing new pictures on Instagram of our "littles"—Conrad, Birdie, Charlotte, and now baby Wills. While these are wonderful benefits of communicating with technology, it's tempting to become consumed by it and live more in the virtual world than in the actual, physical world. But like all temptations, this one can be fought—and overcome—to our benefit.

Be proactive

Joanna Gaines is a busy mother of four, a wife, and business co-owner of Magnolia Homes and the HGTV show *Fixer Upper* along with her husband, Chip Gaines. She said in a recent interview, "When I get home from work, I leave my cell phone in the car. It reminds me to separate work mode from mom mode, clearing space for me to be fully present with my family."[60]

There are a lot of good ideas online (where else?) on how to set technology boundaries for you and your family.

Tips to protect your actual world:

- Protect dinnertime. Put all iPhones in a basket on the counter away from the table.
- Decide on your own boundaries in your home and in your family for screen time. Every day, save at least two hours of non-Internet use.
- Use common courtesy. If you get a phone call you must take, excuse yourself and go into another room or outside so that others don't have to listen to your conversation.
- Realize that it is not imperative that you answer every phone call or text immediately.
- Establish a scheduled break (a Sabbath) from your devices and see if you can go a whole day without them.
- Work on being present to those in your actual presence.

It's good to see our own children learning ways to combat the digital clutter, as I think this is an especially huge challenge for children who are digital natives—technology use comes so easily to them. We're all on a learning curve with technology, but we must be proactive, or we will drown in digital clutter.

> *"The world is too much with us; late and soon, Getting and spending, we lay waste our powers; Little*

we see in Nature that is ours; We have given our hearts away, a sordid boon!"[61]

PRECIOUS CLUTTER

"Clutter in your physical surroundings will clutter your mind and spirit."

– Kaneisha.com

A friend told me, "I am overwhelmed this year with the 'precious clutter' of my mom and dad's earthly goods after their passing this past year." Keepsakes, pictures, and mementos that carry sentiment can take up a lot of physical and emotional space. My piano takes up a lot of space in my office, but right now it's worth it to me, as well as the family pictures in my antique hutch. These things carry emotional weight that right now add joy to my life.

But too much of a good thing can be too much, and our homes can mirror who we are as we hold onto things that represent our past expectations and emotional attachments. While it's comforting and good to honor the past, we cannot live our present life fully when we are focused on what was. Clutter keeps a home from living up to its present potential as well.

There is a fine balance to knowing what to get rid of and what to keep, and as only you are a steward of your things, only you can decide what to do about it. Clutter is individual. I understand the tendency to clutter too well, as I tend to hold onto things, mainly for what they represent to me: A place setting for twenty-four people, waiting for that magical moment when we will all be together again. A silver tea set from our twenty-fifth anniversary celebration. An ideal size of clothing that I hope to get back into. In the back of my mind I think, *I can use this someday.*

I finally boxed up the clothing and let it go, along with the set of dishes. I kept the tea set because I use it at our Christmas tea at church with my daughter and daughters-in-law. Right now, storing it is worth that special time with my girls, but I will hold it loosely and when it's time, I will let it go.

A 2016 profile of buyers and sellers from the Massachusetts Association of Realtors said that when a person age eighteen to fifty-four sells a house, the next home will be larger. If the seller is fifty-five or older, the next house will be smaller. That means that baby boomers are trying to unload a lot of stuff. Not only their own, but their parents' and grandparents' keepsakes as well—and the younger generation doesn't want it.[62] They may say, "Text a picture of it to me," wanting to look before they agree to take something. Usually the final answer is, "No thanks." Sometimes, if it's useful and they want it, we can pass it on. But most of the time? We can't.

After our recent downsizing, Bill and I were left with two storage units (one of which we just emptied). I cringed when I heard a comedian characterize what we're doing: "You know that really ugly stuff we never use? Let's pay a stranger to store it. For years!"

If you are planning a move, this is a good opportunity to pare down. Even if you aren't moving, you can pretend that you are. My friend Brie took one hour every day for several months and went through each room (including drawers and closets) as if she were moving. In the process, she got rid of a lot of excess stuff, and she exclaimed, "It felt so good to purge!" After she had a garage sale, she realized she needed better seating in her living room and bought two great chairs with the money she earned.

Home is a metaphor for ourselves, and as I've stated before, I believe that until we are truly at home with who we are, we struggle with home. Some people are open and welcoming. Some are not, and the differences, although subtle, are striking.

Maybe part of your personal "decluttering" is to cut yourself some slack. Do the best you can, get advice, then apply it. And don't be too hard on yourself. There are a lot of moving parts to keeping a home, and life happens. Illness, unexpected company, children, work deadlines—it can all mess up the best of schedules.

Keeping our homes clean and free of clutter takes work, but with organization and planning, we can make our home into that wonderful place we long to have. The benefits are big.

Here are some simple and practical housekeeping tips:[63]

- Make your bed (teach your kids to make theirs too).
- Clean as you go (pick up during commercials).
- If you take it out, put it away.
- Take fifteen minutes a day to clean something.
- Deal with mail every day.
- Clean and wipe counters daily.
- Don't go to bed with dirty dishes in the sink.
- Keep a bag or box for giveaways.
- Delegate! (Unless you are the only one in the house)

While housework makes our places clean and comfortable, it's important to remember that home is also a place to play. Consider giving yourself permission to relax:

- Take time off (deal with that laundry later)
- Read a good book
- Do something creative, such as a craft
- Make popcorn and watch your favorite show or a movie
- Soak in the tub or give yourself a manicure

"Our homes should inspire us to go out into the world and do great things and then welcome us back for refreshment."

– The Inspired Room

How important is it for you to keep your house clean? With the questions below, discuss with others or for your own insight, reflect on the actual work that your home requires.

- What do I think of when I hear the word "housework"?
- What is good (or bad) about it?
- Is it possible to get out of balance – to make cleaning more important than it should be?
- What is working for me now regarding the work in my home?
- What is not (and how can I address it)?
- What may be a better way of organizing my cleaning and addressing clutter?

Chapter 7

Making Your Home Beautiful

". . . do you know that it's possible (although very, very hard) to create a building that makes you feel the way you do when a loved one smiles at your or when a child holds your hand?"[64]

What makes a home beautiful?

As I write, it is summer. Early this morning I took a walk in the woods behind our house to beat the heat of the day. I came home and entered through the patio door off the deck, standing for a moment to survey the great room, an open concept that includes the kitchen, dining, and living rooms. Bill rearranged the furniture while I was away one day last week, and the jury is still out as to whether this is a good arrangement. I have to admit it has opened up space, and it created a cozy conversation spot for my two red chairs, which we brought from our previous house. The yellow rosebush my son Andy gave me for Mother's Day last year is blooming again, and freshly cut roses in a crystal vase reflect the morning sun from their spot on the dining room table. The whole room radiates.

Yesterday was a cleaning day, and the wide-planked oak floors provide a quiet, timeless setting to the room.

My home feels inviting, comfortable. Dare I say—beautiful?

Making your home beautiful is a creative, personal process

So I ask it again: What makes a home beautiful? Beauty doesn't necessarily mean a perfectly decorated house, attractive architectural design, or even cleanliness—although all those things help. I believe instead that having a beautiful home is an ongoing, creative, and personal process. It takes cleaning, maintenance, and stewardship. It may take bravery, risking mistakes.

A beautiful home has integrity. It is reflective of its owner, not pretentious; but as we work with it, it becomes a place to breathe and dream of making a better life, a better us. Annemarie Dzanbo described it this way: "Home is the story of who we are and a collection of all the things we love." Along with, of course, practical furnishings to help us in our daily lives.

We bring into our homes our personalities and the sometimes-meandering path which has taken us to where we are. The structure and location of your place will vary but creating your dream home starts with you. Dreams don't work unless you work to make them happen.

The highest calling of a home is to provide the best environment possible to help those who live in it to have a good, beautiful life. Home is meant to support your life. Home is a place in which to develop people of character, generosity, and goodness, including your children and yourself. Your home can be a safe and beautiful place to hold you and those you love.

> *"Architecture is the bones, Decor is the heart, and art is the soul of a room."*
>
> *– Terri Lind Davis*

Work with what you have

> *"The essence of interior design will always be about people and how they live.*
>
> *It is about the realities of what makes for an attractive, civilized, meaningful environment. Not about fashion or what's in or what's out. This is not an easy job."*
>
> *– Albert Hadley*

Now let's get practical.

No matter what your house is like in its roughest form, no matter its shape or its appraised value—it is the material you have to develop into your own beautiful home.

My husband and I moved into a new house this year that is drastically different from our previous one of logs and beams and wood and stone and wide porches. Our new house is smaller, in a modern, contemporary style, and it is in a housing development. We have close neighbors on both sides of us. Very close.

I did not immediately love this house. The way the doors closed bothered me; they didn't feel as solid as the doors in our log home. While I love people, I also cherish my privacy, and I have had to work to find my "spots."

Still, I am choosing to embrace the new place, the new house, the new neighborhood as I've chosen to consciously look for the good. I am finding it.

Our goal was downsizing, a task that requires intention and persistence. We sold our log home furnished, which meant leaving three bedroom sets, our dining room table that opened up to seat twenty-one, my husband's large antique walnut desk, and my baby grand piano in the loft. As we tried to find things that would work in this new place, I felt as if I was on a search to gather missing pieces of my life. I looked for a piano on Craigslist. We looked for a dining room set, and we immediately bought one, as I had an irrational fear that something bad would happen if I didn't have a place for family meals. As it turned out, that hurried purchase was a mistake. The table wasn't big enough and didn't have a leaf where we could expand it to include family and friends. We recently sold it and got another set from the Habitat Re-Store that fits our needs.

If you are downsizing or moving into a new house, take your time in choosing the furnishings. If something is meaningful to you and carries comfortable memories, find a way to keep it. In our new house, I realized how much we would miss the generous built-in cabinets that held our family dishes and seasonal serving pieces. Bill went on a search and found an old buffet in a secondhand store that had seen its best years. He went to work refinishing and staining it, and he secured its doors and drawers with new knobs. It's a beautiful piece. Although many boxes of our old dish sets went to the thrift store or garage sales, what remains now has a home.

With work and experimentation, this house is beginning to look and feel like our place. What I'm learning, however, is that it's not possible to fit a square peg into a round hole. This is not a log cabin in the woods; it's a contemporary house in a neighborhood, and all the dreaming in the world won't change its basic structure and design. We may have to stand back and analyze what this new place requires, rather than trying to make it look like our previous home or someone else's.

Take a clear-eyed look to see what you have to work with, in terms of budget, location, and existing structure. Furnishing your home is something like picking your wardrobe. You can go at it with a haphazard guess as to what clothes and accessories to buy and wear, or with some education and advice, you can make thoughtful choices based on need, lifestyle, and budget. One of my favorite TV shows is *What Not to Wear,* a funny yet educational take on how or how not to dress. We can be given a budget to stick to, an understanding of body type and lifestyle, and then we choose the best way to present ourselves.

It's important to understand that in our desire to make our home beautiful, less can be more. We can over-accessorize in our dress, and we can also over-decorate our homes. There should be a cohesiveness to how our homes look—not things just thrown together. Making your dream home starts with a realistic assessment of what you have to work with. A factory-made home can be made uniquely yours. An RV can be made uniquely yours.

Alice Gentry, a woman in her late sixties who barely scrapes by on social security, has qualified to live in Opportunity Village in one of the tiny homes being built in Eugene, Oregon. Right now, she is living in a sixty-four-square foot bungalow. Some University of Oregon students are raising funds, through volunteer labor and materials, to help Alice get into a 180-square-foot house with its own kitchen, electricity, and running water and bathtub. Alice is excited about the possibility of getting a real home, especially a bathtub, which to her represents a solid sense of home, of ownership. She also wants a place to welcome others. Lyndsey Deaton, one of the graduate students involved in this project, says, "Part of home and having a place of your own is the ability to engage and welcome other people. That's a privilege of someone who has a home; that you can invite other people to it; that you can extend that generosity."[65] Alice's house is small, but it's beautiful.

Some of us don't possess that interior designer gene others have, but we can get inspiration from others. My sister-in-law Lila has the eye of an expert and knows just what to do with a basket here, a certain rug there, to pull it all together. And go with your instincts—they're not fatal. You can always repaint or move a piece of furniture if something doesn't work. We may think we can't afford elegant furnishings, so we give up and exist with what we have in a sort of uneasy truce. But living with limits offers us a chance to be creative. Shop yard sales and thrift stores for that special find. Or you can sell what you don't want, online or at a yard sale, and replace it with just the perfect table or piece. One benefit of cleaning your house is that it gives you time and space to "play" with your home; to rearrange furniture or take out unnecessary items or clutter. Getting rid of what we don't need or what doesn't fit is the first step to seeing what we do need. And we can learn. There are home decorating books or magazines; home shows on television; decorating ideas on Pinterest.

Stopping in at open houses can also inspire us. Creating your own beautiful home begins with creative puttering. Start with one room, one corner, and see what you can do to improve it.

Let a house be what it is. But you can work with what you have to make it beautiful.

> *"The foolish man seeks happiness in the distance . . . the wise grows it under his feet."*
>
> – *James Oppenheim*[66]

MOVE IN, EMOTIONALLY

Alexandra Stoddard observed that most of us live in houses that were designed for someone else. So it follows that when we move into a home physically, we must also move in emotionally. That may take some work. She writes, "We are housing *our* lives now, and that cannot be dictated by abstract principles that say a living room must be a living room, a dining room must be used as a dining room . . . Think of the inside of your house as your soul and the outside architecture as something like your bone structure, your genetic inheritance. The shell of the house is only an introduction to who we are. It is inside where we express ourselves, filling space with the personally meaningful, beautiful, and symbolic that affirm our individuality."[67]

To move in emotionally where we are, some of us must grieve the loss of our previous home and the life we lived there. It's important to acknowledge the loss so that we don't get stuck in looking back. Then we can move on to celebrate where we are.

Moving in emotionally begins with gratitude. Being grateful for what was and grateful for what is. I miss the walks behind my previous houses. I miss the place on my covered porch as I watched the sun set. That was my spot, and now I must find a new one. I'm grateful for what was. But I will also look for what is and choose to be grateful for that too.

Although we are within the city limits now, we are backed up to Forest Service land that will never be developed, and we can look out our oversized sliding glass doors off the great room onto a trail through the trees. We see many birds and wildlife from here. It's different from my old spot, but it's a good one.

The old places and spots I loved are gone from me now—and the life I lived there is gone too. Sometimes I think of the old places, and when I indulge myself, I lament. It isn't only the home, the house, I miss. I miss the old voices and the presence of those who are gone from me, by death or distance or alienation. *I miss them.* And I miss who I was in those places.

We miss the oddest things. After the children of Israel left slavery in Egypt, they missed the leeks and the garlic. If you are still in love with your previous place, you must acknowledge it and then find a way to let it go. To love where we are, our focus must become on what is, not what was. It isn't helpful to look back, as we are not going that way.

We can choose to see the negative, or we can see what we have as a gift from God that we receive gratefully. Gratitude changes everything—most of all us. We can embrace where we are and look to see the positive in it.

"Even when I enter a space that I have to design for a client, I listen to what the space says – the walls, the windows. You can't change what that space wants to be."

– Lella Vignelli

Set your imagination free

"We must first see the vision in order to realize it; we must have the ideal, or we cannot approach it."

– Laura Ingalls Wilder[68]

The fun and creative aspect about your home is that it is so uniquely *yours*. No other place belongs to you like this does. So dream! Let your home reflect what is important to you. Let your personality shine through and show your sense of humor and playfulness. Let it showcase what matters to you. If there are certain hobbies or activities that you love, incorporate them somehow.

William Morris, a poet, artist, and designer in the late 1800s, wrote, "Have nothing in your house that you do not believe to be useful, or believe to be beautiful."[69] And, I would add, "meaningful."

You can create a beautiful home even if it wasn't born beautiful by using what you have. Take another look at what you have in another room, or in storage, that may work in a different place in your house. Dropping by local thrift shops or garage sales can help you find that perfect treasure.

There is nothing like fresh flowers on a gleaming, cleaned-off table or counter to add beauty to a home.

Splurge occasionally and get some fresh roses or peonies or tulips from the grocery store.

Emily Henderson, of HGTV's *Secrets of a Stylist,* gives good advice regarding the importance of color. Her advice is to be careful not to have more than three or four brown items—such as darker floors, carpet, leather furniture, etc.—in one place, as these tend to darken a room. There's a fine line between cozy and oppressive. Take another look to see if you may be missing a pop of color that could add interest to your room.

It is the subtle, individual touches that add beauty to a home. Lighting. A stack of old books. White candles. Music.

> *"Homes without personality are a series of walled enclosures with furniture standing around in them. Other houses are filled with things of little intrinsic value, even with much that is shabby and yet they have that inviting atmosphere."*
>
> *–Emily Post*

Consider your own home and the bigger picture of your life. How can your home make room for dreams for you and your family? How does your home facilitate growth and creativity?

Your home's mission statement

> *"Great design is eliminating all unnecessary details."*
>
> *–Minh D. Tran*

Your home tells a story—your story, a continuing tale in which you are actively involved. What is the story that you want to tell? What is the theme or purpose of your home? Is it apparent, even in subtle ways? If not, embracing simplicity may help.

Simplicity has to do with focus and can help us articulate our home's mission statement. I'm not simple, and most people I know do not live simple lives. Yet there is a hunger, a longing somehow to be there. The word *simplicity* may throw us off, because the very concept seems foreign to us. We are blessed by so many things, so many options, and amid clutter and complexity, it can be hard to see the focus of our home. Jesus told Martha, "One thing is needed." Perhaps the focus of our home has to do with our priorities, so a better question to ask is, *What is my home's priority, and is it living up to it?*

Not far from where I live is a spectacularly beautiful mansion. It was originally built to be a home. Now it's an art gallery and a museum. Sam Hill, an entrepreneur at the turn of the century, built it in 1907 on 5,300 acres of land along the Columbia River. He dreamed of establishing a Quaker farming community and a stately home for his wife, his son, and his mentally ill daughter. The mansion is now known as Maryhill Art Museum. Despite his intentions to build a home for his family, Sam Hill was an unabashed philanderer. His wife left after a decade of this and moved back East with the children, so his beautiful home, filled with art, was left empty. The towering building features columns of architectural beauty, exquisite art, and sculptures, including some by Rodin. But the beautiful house is not a beautiful home. It's a place about objects, not a place of refuge or joy or family. It is a beautiful shell with no spark of fire or spirit.

What makes a home beautiful? You do. You are beautiful—a one-of-a-kind person with a one-of-a-kind story to tell through your home. Your home exists and should function for *you* and those in your family who live there.

By your own hands, your own creativity, you can make your home beautiful. Solomon observed, "The wise woman builds her house, but the foolish pulls it down with her hands."[70]

> *"I wonder if the real measure of 'home' is the degree to which you can leave it alone. Maybe appreciating a house means knowing when to stop decorating. Maybe you've never really lived there until you've thrown its broken pieces in the garbage. Maybe learning how to be out in the big world isn't the epic journey everyone thinks it is. Maybe that's actually the easy part. The hard part is what's right in front of you. The hard part is learning how to hold the title to your very existence, to own not only property, but also your life. The hard part is learning not just how to be but mastering the nearly impossible art of how to be at home."*[71]

Walk into your home and try to see it with fresh eyes. Go from room to room, taking notes. Ask yourself:

- What do I and my family need from this place?
- Is it fulfilling its potential?
- What do I most like about it? How can I enhance that?
- What is not working? What are practical ways to change that?
- What are the positive aspects of living where I am? (Rehearse them!)

"We are haunted by an ideal life, and it is because we have within us the beginning and the possibility of it."

– Unknown

Think about what needs happen for you to move in, emotionally. Here are some practical suggestions:

- Take out a membership in the local library (invest yourself locally).
- Make it a point to attend local events, such as art shows, book signings, and music events.
- Host a coffee and dessert or appetizer gathering to get to know your new neighbors.

"Some people look for a beautiful place. Others make a place beautiful."

– Hazrat Inayat Khan

Chapter 8

The Gift of Hospitality

"The real histories of families aren't the records of births, deaths, and marriages.

They are the stories told after dessert, when the coffee's been served and everyone's too full to move."

– Frederick Waterman[72]

When I was in the fifth grade, I decided it would be fun to have an overnight Halloween party at our house for all the kids at our country school (about a dozen). I personally talked to their parents, telling my schoolmates to bring their costumes, PJs, and toothbrushes. The kids were excited about having a hot dog roast, then having my dad drive us around to various houses afterward to trick or treat. The night before the big party, I thought I had better let my mother know what was happening.

Mother was astounded. "We are absolutely *not* having a party here!" She and my father had made plans to go out of town and were leaving us in the capable hands of Mrs. Moore, a neighbor who occasionally babysat us. One of the most embarrassing moments of my life was having to tell all the school parents that the party was off.

Maybe hospitality has always been easy to me, as I like to have people in. But it has taken me a lifetime to fully appreciate what hospitality is and what it isn't.

True hospitality: a warm welcome

True hospitality is more than just having someone to your house for dinner. Hospitality is about going out of your way to welcome people into your *life*. It's an open-door, open-heart philosophy.

I have a sign near my entrance: *Welcome Home.* You probably have one like it. I just took a walk through our neighborhood and smiled when I saw a mat in front of a home that said *Stay Away*. Someone has a sense of humor—or maybe he or she really does not want visitors.

Our homes have the actual, physical potential to welcome us, and they have the same potential to welcome those who come to see us. My *Welcome Home* sign out front is a little askew, as I have it propped between a couple of plants, but I do mean it: *Welcome to my home!*

But welcome takes more than a cute sign. Walk outside of your house and take a hard, objective look at the front of it. What is your first impression? The first impression of your house is like your home's business card or your website. Whether the front of your house features a simple window box or small crate of herbs, or whether it's a more elaborate yard and garden, it sets the tone for your home.

Take time to observe others' entrances and see what you find appealing and what you don't. It doesn't take much to set a tone of welcome. Perhaps it's a bench or a chair out front. Flowers. A freshly swept entrance. A clutter-free front porch.

I like flags out front, as they help identify who we are and what we celebrate: the American flag for patriotic days; my "Hallelujah" flag for Easter; Bill's "Oregon Duck" flag when football season starts. Some people prefer a minimalist, neat approach. Use your own creativity and style to welcome and inspire others, and maybe most importantly of all, create an entrance to welcome yourself.

The heart of true hospitality is understanding that hospitality is a gift we can give others—a spiritual gift. True hospitality is not some razzle-dazzle show meant to impress, but a giving of yourself to see that another is made comfortable.

> *"The heart of hospitality is when people leave your home they should feel better about themselves, not better about you."*
>
> – *Shauna Niequest,* The Power of the Living Room[73]

Growing in hospitality

The best hospitality is easy, not forced. There's an openness to it—not a defensive stance of, *Oh, you're seeing my mess. You'll think I'm a terrible person and housekeeper. It's not always like this. (Sometimes it's worse!)*

Hospitality can seem intimidating. But, hospitality is as simple as noticing people. Smiling. Saying, "Hello. How are you?" Hospitality can be as revolutionary and yet as doable as taking time to introduce yourself or someone you are with to someone new. Hospitality is about bringing people into your circle. "What the world needs now . . . is love, sweet love!" And we can give it, if only we take a moment or two.

When we go a step further and invite someone into our home, something dramatic and expansive happens to us. We discover the exquisite gift of hospitality. And it's a gift that comes back to us: the writer of Proverbs observed, "Your own soul is nourished when you are kind."[74]

My mother-in-law, Betty, developed the art of making her home a welcoming place for family, friends, or anyone who dropped by. Once after a houseful of people left, I was in the kitchen helping her clean up. As she put away the extra cookies and wiped off the counter, she mused, "The house always seems happy after company leaves. There's a glow. There's a warmth that stays." I have seen that intangible quality too. Hospitality has staying power. It magnifies the home; the atmosphere is elevated; we are more conscious of our manners. We listen more.

For some, hospitality comes easily. For others, the thought of "entertaining" strikes terror in the heart. *Is my house clean enough? Is this food good enough? Is my house nice enough?* But we can learn hospitality and grow in it. The first thing we learn is the difference between entertaining and hospitality. *Entertaining is about making yourself look good; hospitality is about making others feel good.*

So where do we start?

- **Start small.** Hospitality is giving out of the time and resources you have. It means taking the initiative to invite people into your space, which can mean making a coffee date with someone, or stopping to ask your new neighbor her name and welcome her to the area. It means having an awareness of others, of their needs.

- **It takes a certain recklessness.** There is never a perfect time for hospitality. Life happens. Be easy on yourself. There may be times you can't reach out. But remember that everyone needs a friend. Some may not respond to you, but some will. Reaching out is a risk. It's worth taking.
- **Watch how other people do it.** I've learned everything I know about hospitality by watching my friends: Caro, Patti, Char, Kitty, and others—you know who you are! Now I am learning fresh ways of hospitality from my daughters-in-law, my nieces, and my younger friends. We can borrow ideas from anyone.
- **Master a meal or two.** If you feel comfortable with what you are preparing, hospitality is easier. It helps to try out a new recipe on yourself or your family first.
- **Simplify.** Serve appetizers or have coffee and dessert.
- **Let others help.** If your guests ask, "What can I bring?" take them up on their offer. It can be wonderful to taste others' contributions. There are ways to simplify hospitality that don't require a lot of work. One couple I know made dinner reservations at a restaurant for a party of eight and invited their friends, letting them know it was no-host. After dinner, the couple invited them all over for coffee and dessert for further conversation. It was a delightful evening, and not a lot of work for the host.

Most of all, hospitality is making other people feel accepted and welcomed in your space. If you are comfortable, others will be comfortable. It's not about you or your reputation as a hostess or host. I've had some hospitality disasters, including one less-than-memorable evening when I had a houseful of guests for dinner and decided to try out a couple of new recipes. It felt like a slow motion horror movie as it seemed that everything went from bad to worse. Finally, I laughed at myself along with everyone else, and served coffee and dessert, which ended the evening on a sweet note. I doubt my friends even remember the salad with the too-tart dressing or the overly done roast.

We can learn fresh ways of hospitality from others. When we were first married and living in San Francisco, Bill and I were invited to another young couple's apartment for dinner. Both were busy professionals who worked in the city. When we arrived at their apartment at the appointed time, the raw ingredients for dinner were on the counter—chicken, vegetables, and apples for an apple pie. They served appetizers and beverages, and then we watched as they consulted the recipes and made dinner, and I helped by peeling the apples for the apple pie.

I still have Dick and Diane's recipes from that evening, as I copied them while we waited for dinner to be done. I remember being amazed at the whole thing, because I had thought that hospitality meant arriving at someone's home to experience a well-put-together meal, ready or nearly ready. This was not their style; and I saw that for them, it was all about the preparation, the laughter. Pour the wine, break the bread, and talk. And listen. It was a perfect meal, a perfect evening. Dick and Diane made room in their busy lives to invite us in. And we were grateful.

Hospitality is an offering of self. We can grow in it, as well as model it to our own children. The other day as we left our son and daughter-in-law's home, three-year-old Conrad came out to tell us good-bye and urged us to "Come over, come over!" His parents are hospitable, and he has learned by watching.

Hospitality is a mind-set

The mind-set of hospitality is one of reaching out, not settling for the same-old, same-old routine and friends and family, but reaching out to new people, to people beyond our comfort zone. What keeps us from hospitality? It may be our feeling that "I'm just not good at it. It's not my gift." Or "I don't want to be bothered." We may think we have to live up to some invisible standard that we can't attain, or that we don't have time for it.

There is never the perfect time for hospitality. Some of the busiest people I know are the most hospitable. My friend LeeAnn and her husband travel all over the world with various ministries and business and have a large extended family. But when she is home even a day or two, she is always up to inviting a new friend over, or a cherished older one, to "catch up."

My mother had to learn hospitality, as she grew up within a tight circle of herself, her mother and brother, and only a few trusted, longtime friends. When she moved to the farm and married my father, who never knew a stranger, she grew in hospitality. Our home was always open to others. Hospitality begins with yourself and your circle of family. Then the circle widens.

"Happy is the house that shelters a friend."

– Ralph Waldo Emerson

What about solitude? I need my space!

Is it possible to crave solitude and community all at the same time? Absolutely. I'm a people person, but it seems to me that solitude is an essential ingredient to true community. And we don't find solitude; we create it. We must fight for it. It takes deliberate intention to be still, to bring our noisy selves into God's presence. Jesus did that a lot, despite being immersed with his disciples and the crowds, the constant controversies and the overwhelming needs of ordinary people who swarmed him.

Without a doubt, there are times for privacy and boundaries. In fact, the truest hospitality comes out of that sheltered place. If you don't have the time and place to be rejuvenated, it's impossible to give out. To truly give, we must have times to gather ourselves.

My dear friend whose home was filled with people for many years in ministry settings realized that as her husband aged, he was no longer up to the large crowds they had been used to having. But she found other ways to give. She would invite a friend or two to go out to lunch with her at a restaurant. She would also bake cookies and share them with her neighbors. She took time to visit friends in a nursing home. She kept the true spirit of hospitality.

When we lived in Salem and were on staff with a church, our lives were full. We had four small boys, and life was a blur of baseball, soccer, church, and school activities. We lived in a neighborhood with many young families, and our backyard was the best one: Bill had built a treehouse, the perfect gathering spot for kids. Our home was kid central. We loved it, but at times it became too much. We learned to make certain days "family days," so when neighborhood kids knocked on our door, we could say, "Sorry, we can't play today. It's Family Day." We needed time to be just us.

Jesus is our best example of what it means to be hospitable. He turned the water into wine. He let children clamber on his lap. He provided food for the people in the countryside. But he also frequently escaped from people to be still and listen to the Father. And we can do the same.

People today are starved for the ministry of hospitality. In our culture of technological isolation and frequent moves, we need people, and people need us. And we need God's love to love them.

The wonder of it is that our Lord is so accessible to us through the most common things of life. A cup of water for a thirsty worker outside on a hot day. Taking time for coffee for a friend new to the area. Listening to a child. Texting a Scripture of hope and healing to a friend, knowing she is going through a rough patch.

Hospitality isn't that hard. It simply means to be aware of others, and because freely we have received, freely we can give. Sometimes we hold off inviting someone over, especially if we know they are a great cook or hostess. A friend who was a well-known chef with his own television show remarked that no one ever invited him for dinner. He said he wouldn't have cared if it was just soup and bread. He would just love to have been invited to someone's home.

Hospitality is good for everyone—it's good for those you reach out to, and it's good for you too. Parties are just plain fun, and a good party brings joy. It's been said that the kingdom of God is a party. It sure is!

Garrit Dawson wrote, "I imagine that when [the disciples] first began to divide five loaves and two fish among thousands of people, the disciples gave little tiny pieces. They tried to make the food go as far as it would. But as their supply did not diminish, I envision their giving away larger and larger pieces. They fairly tossed huge hunks of bread, great slices of fish. What began as a hesitant division in anticipation of want ended with an expansive excess of food for all. This was no grim religious business. Jesus played host to a feast in the desert. And I feel sure it was an hour filled with celebrative delight."[75]

In the truest spiritual sense of the word, hospitality is a gift that can change the world as it breaks down barriers and becomes a visible sign of love. St. Benedict said, "Hospitality maintains a prominence in the living Christian tradition . . . the guest represents Christ and has a claim on the welcome and care of the community."

"My little children, let us not love in word or in tongue, but in deed and in truth."

– 1 John 3:18

Hospitality: bringing the outsiders in

"Do not forget to entertain strangers, for by so doing some have unwittingly entertained angels."

– Hebrews 13:2, NKJV

Hospitality gets to be its most fun and unexpected here. Jesus reminded us that what we do to "the least of these," we do to him.[76] The writer of Hebrews threw out the revolutionary idea that there are strangers among us who may really be heavenly visitors—angels. And we can welcome them. True spiritual hospitality is about seeing someone outside our circle and opening our hearts and our homes to him or her.

It was a stormy and frigid late afternoon with near-blizzard conditions on the plains of northern Montana. My father had taken me and most of my siblings into town for piano lessons and shopping. Only my mother and my brother Dan were home, and Mother started to worry about us as the roads were icy and snow was blowing, making it hard to see. The wind made mournful violin sounds as it howled around the corners of the old farmhouse. It was near Christmas time, and my mother had been on a cleaning frenzy. She sat down to wait for us and surveyed her hard work with satisfaction. Everything shone, floors freshly waxed. There was a stew simmering on the back of the stove, supper ready for the family. Those moments didn't happen very often at our house, but there it was, and Mother savored it.

That's when someone knocked at the back door. Mother opened it to a strange sight. At first, she couldn't tell who was standing there in a mask of snow and ice.

"Oh—it's Robert!" Mother finally exclaimed.

Robert Norton lived down the road about five miles from us, in a little shack he shared with his mother. Folks in the community called him "Snortin' Norton" due to a cleft palate that had never been repaired, which made talking and controlling his saliva difficult for him. Neighbors said Snortin' Norton was "not quite right" mentally. It wasn't that folks were intentionally mean to Robert.

They did charitable things for him. But there's a difference between that and acceptance.

Now he stood at Mother's back door, saliva and mucous frozen, so covered by snow and ice that he was nearly unrecognizable.

Mother brought Robert in and ran to get warm washcloths and towels. My brother Dan helped her as she gently cleaned Robert's face. His boots left muddy puddles all over the freshly waxed floor. He mumbled that his car had careened off the road a mile away. He'd walked all the way here, searching for help to dig it out of the mounding snow.

"Of course," Mother assured him. "The family will be home soon, and Gunder and the boys will help you. But let's get you out of those wet things."

It was then that she noticed Robert staring around the warm and welcoming room with delight.

"Oh, Robert," she said. "Would you like some warm stew?"

His eyes lit up. "Sure!" he blurted.

Mother reached for an everyday mug near the stove. Suddenly, she stopped and hung it back on the rack. A sense of the holy came over her as she reached instead for her best china and set a place at the wobbly kitchen table. *It occurred to her that maybe the Lord himself . . . or maybe one of his angels . . . was here in her kitchen, having stew.*

When she told us later about Robert's visit, it was with a catch in her voice and shining eyes. "Do not forget to entertain strangers, for by so doing some have unwittingly entertained angels."[77]

"He drew a circle that shut me out –
Heretic, rebel, a thing to flout
But love and I had the wit to win;
We drew a circle and took him in!"
– Edwin Markham, from "Outwitted"(1852–1940)

Hospitality: it's about food

"Homes should mean something to us humans. They are a basic instinct. A home, with a life that centers only on food and sleep, is not really a home, it's a house. Beauty and graciousness, joy of living, being used in every part, these are the things that make a house a home."[78]

Let's face it. People get hungry. Food is a common, human need, and through preparing it, we make the powerful statement that life is to be lived; that nourishment encourages us onward, invites us to life.

There is something about the comfort of a home-cooked meal and a table set that says, "I have prepared this for you." It cheers us in the best of times; and it pulls us forward, even in the worst of times.

I vividly remember the potluck in our church basement after my dad's funeral service. It was a Montana January day, skies clear blue, and zero degrees outside. I sat at a crowded table in a roomful of old friends and family members. There were scalloped potatoes and ham. Erna's baked beans, from scratch. Aunt Emma's light-than-feather rolls. Apple pie. Comfortable, home-cooked food lovingly prepared by my aunts, by women in the church and in the community. Dad would have loved it.

It was the first time after losing my father that I had the faintest hope that maybe we'd be all right now; that maybe life would go on.

> *"Home is where the stove is. When I think of all the places I've lived, I think of what I cooked in the kitchen: cheese tarts in Cambridge, beet soup in Berkeley, and shrimp curry in Singapore. Home is where I sauté the garlic and chop the onions, where the frying pan makes music.*
>
> *– JoAnn Passerello Deck*

Creative ways to incorporate hospitality

- Think outside the box. Maybe hospitality means packing a picnic lunch and taking a trek through the woods.
- Know someone experiencing a stressful day? Call in advance and take a meal for them in disposable containers.
- Invite fellow sports fans in to enjoy a game.
- Celebrate ordinary days: the first day of the month; a good report card; the end of a semester at school.

Consider the place that hospitality has in your life and in your home. Are there ways you can grow in hospitality? List them and try to incorporate a few soon.

- How are you offering hospitality to yourself and your own family right now?
- How can you prepare yourself and your home to be a more open place for others?

Chapter 9

Home: Your Safe Place

"To some this world may seem like no place to bring up a child.

And in some respect, they are right.

But we take that risk anyway with the comforting knowledge that it is not for this world that we prepare them."[79]

My brother John and I were playing in the barn one warm afternoon when I spotted something colorful nestled in the hay. I thought it was a belt, or a suspender, and at eight years old and innocent, I bent over to pick it up. I realized with a start that it was a snake. I had been with my older sister when she was bitten by a rattlesnake not far from that spot, and since then I'd gone out of my way to avoid snakes. Terrified, I ran for the door, but standing in the doorway of the barn was our huge Black Angus bull—not known for his friendly ways. He stood, lowering his head at me, refusing to budge. I was stuck. I couldn't go back; I couldn't go forward. I screamed with all my might.

Johnny came to my rescue and chased the bull away. I bolted past him and ran for the house, threw open the screen door and sat on the floor, trembling. I may have set a world record for fastest eight-year-old. Mother was baking cinnamon rolls; she had Nat King Cole playing on the stereo. What a relief! I was safe. I was *home.*

I am grateful that as a child, I felt safe at home. There are many who do not, as some homes are not safe.

Frederick Buechner wrote, "The grace of God means something like: Here is your life. You might never have been, but you are because the party wouldn't have been complete without you. Here is the world. Beautiful and terrible things will happen. Don't be afraid. I am with you. Nothing can ever separate us. It's for you I created the universe. I love you. There's only one catch. Like any other gift, the gift of grace can be yours if only you'll reach out to take it. Maybe reaching out and taking it is a gift, too."[80]

I love this quote because it is honest and yet comforting. Is this not why we have homes? Why we try to create a consistent place of comfort and nourishment and grace? Because along with the reality of a hostile world is the paradox of so much beauty and joy that surrounds us. Home can be a safe place to celebrate the best things of life.

What makes a home a safe? I believe a safe home provides five elements:

- Protection
- Nourishment
- Celebration
- Comfort
- Grace

A SAFE HOME OFFERS PROTECTION

> *"We comfort ourselves by reliving memories of protection. Something closed must retain our memories, while leaving them their original value as images. Memories of the outside world will never have the same tonality as those of home and, by recalling these memories, we add to our store of dreams; we are never real historians, but always near poets, and our emotion is perhaps nothing but an expression of a poetry that was lost."*
>
> – *Gaston Bachelard,* The Poetics of Space

Throughout history, we humans have been driven to make homes that shelter and provide safety for ourselves and those we love. Home may be a nomadic tent; a hut of mud and grass; a place of wood and rock or fiberglass. Regardless, we try. Sometimes we spectacularly fail. Sometimes we do it right. Some of us must learn what it means to make home a safe place.

As I write, many in our neighborhood are having new roofs put on their houses because last winter's epic snowstorm caused a great deal of damage. A house needs a strong roof to withstand four to five feet of snow. And we need strong homes to withstand a hostile world, homes that will provide a zone of safety.

Not long ago, my husband and I spent time volunteering in a city dump in Mexico where many families live, scratching out an existence by repurposing garbage and discarded items. Out of what others had thrown away, they built homes for themselves and their families. I was struck by the commonality that no matter where we live, no matter our level of income, we all need a home of safety and protection.

Protection means, *"This is my house. My place. I can come here and be safe. I can close the door and know that those in authority will see that no evil will harm me."*

Protection means there is someone or something present to welcome us and watch over us. Even our memories can offer that sense of protection and welcome. My sister Judy, who lives alone after years of marriage and raising children, says that when she comes home from work to her house, she is welcomed home by various walls where she hangs important reminders of who she is: her Montana wall; her pictures-of-her-children wall; her civic wall (reminding her of work in the community that she was involved in for so many years). Judy says, "I am not lonely, just 'lone.'" She has frequent visits from family and friends, but she appreciates the quietness—and even her morning ritual of reading the paper with her cat in her lap.

A SAFE HOME IS A PLACE TO BE NOURISHED

> *"Food brings people together on many different levels. It's the nourishment of the soul and body; it's truly love."*
>
> *–Giada De Laurentiis*

> *"If the home is a body, the table is the heart, the beating center, the sustainer of life and health."*[81]

Home is so much about food. Our memories of home are often tied up with sitting around the table with family members. Everyone gets hungry—and the table is a place to take some time to connect with those we love. Maybe the most powerful and radical thing we can do at home is to provide consistent dinners together, which provide emotional as well as physical nourishment. A recent statistic stated that Americans spend more than 40 percent of their food budgets on meals outside the home.[82] I understand why—I'll admit that after spending a lifetime putting together family meals with five active children and providing gatherings for all kinds of people in my house, one of my favorite things to make is "reservations"! But I am convinced more than ever that providing consistent meals in the home, especially when we have children, is a powerful way to create an atmosphere of safety and predictability.

Eating together at home also has enormous benefits, as recent research has shown. Anne Fishel, cofounder of The Family Dinner Project,[83] offers excellent resources and suggestions for practical ways to enhance family dinners. As a family therapist and researcher in North America, Europe, and Australia, she has become convinced that sitting down for a nightly meal is great for the brain, the body, and the spirit. Other researchers have found that for young children, dinnertime conversation boosts vocabulary even more than being read to. For school-age children, regular mealtime is a more powerful predictor of high achievement scores than time spent in school, doing homework, playing sports, or doing art. Adolescents who ate family meals five to seven times a week were twice as likely to get A's in school as those who ate dinner with their families fewer than two times a week.[84]

Nutritional benefits also are high, as children who eat regular family dinners consume more fruits and vegetables and fewer fried foods and soft drinks. (However, research has shown an association between TV-watching during dinner and overweight children.) An even more powerful study has shown that regular family dinners lower high-risk teenage behaviors such as smoking, binge drinking, marijuana use, violence, and school problems, while lowering the risk of depression. In a recent study, kids who had been victims of cyberbullying bounced back more readily if they regularly ate dinner with their family.[85]

How simple, yet how radical it is to provide for ourselves and others a place that is safe and nourishing! When Jesus and his disciples were in the room where they celebrated Passover, he promised them: "I go to prepare a place for you."[86] To know that Jesus is preparing a place for us is a comforting thought. And we too can prepare a nourishing place for ourselves and others in our home.

We set the table: "Here. Welcome! This is for you. Stop and be nourished, be comforted." Taking a bit of time to set the table doesn't take a lot; a placemat, the necessities of silverware, napkin, drink, adding just a touch or two: a flower in a vase, a lighted candle. Sometimes the sketchiest meal of soup or sandwiches is improved by setting a nice table. Every home is different, with different needs depending on where we are in life. It may be that the best family meal for you is breakfast. What matters is eating together.

Last year when Bill and I visited the Sea of Galilee, I studied the hillside, trying to imagine the crowds of people who came looking for Jesus to heal them—the blind, the lame, the questioning ones. And Jesus did heal them, with his touch and his words. But as the days went by, Jesus was concerned that they were also just plain hungry, and through a miracle of breaking loaves of bread and fish, he fed the people physically as well as spiritually.[87]

We can do that too. In our own small way, we offer consistent, needed nourishment, and it will be multiplied and remembered.

> *"The homeliest tasks get beautiful if loving hands do them."*
>
> *– Louisa May Alcott*

A SAFE HOME IS A PLACE TO CELEBRATE

> *"Food was celebration, conversation, and nourishment. The table is where the big decisions of the family are made, and all the arguing takes place."*
>
> *– Adrian Trigiani*

Laughter and joy, filling our place, are signs that we are safe at home. Home provides an easy ability to laugh at oneself, to not take oneself too seriously. People can relax around you, not worried about stepping on hidden landmines.

Birthday celebrations are great opportunities to show tangible love to one special person. One family we know has a tradition of going around the table expressing what they appreciate about the birthday person before he or she blows out the candles on the cake. Even a certain number of candles is a beautiful offering of gratitude for being able to love a certain person for a specific number of years. (Even though some of us may have to call in the fire department when there are too many candles!)

The real truth is that it's the ordinary that is so special, and it is the ordinary that we can celebrate. A good report card, the first day of the month, the beginning or ending of summer, a spur-of-the-moment adventure in your own city, a special accomplishment that calls for a pop of the cork of sparkling cider or champagne—life is full of opportunities to celebrate the ordinary. All we need to do is take them.

A SAFE HOME OFFERS COMFORT

> *"Comfort to me is a room that works for you and your guests. It's deep upholstered furniture. It's also knowing that if someone pulls up a chair for a talk, the whole room doesn't fall apart."*[88]

Do you have places in your home where you can relax—and fully be yourself? What about for others? Is your home a comfortable place for those in your family as well as visitors?

How we all long for and need comfort in the world! The truth is that we are all refugees needing safe places along the way. Although I have traveled a good deal in my life and still do, I get homesick. What is it that I miss? Even if my husband is with me, I miss the familiarity of things. My own comfortable bed, and the sliding door that lets in the cool breeze. My books. My piano. Pictures and reminders of my people. I know (most of the time!) where things are. I know when I pad out to my driveway in my red-plaid fleece robe at 7:30 in the morning, my newspaper will be there. My husband will have already made coffee, French roast.

This is the magic and power of a safe home—it's the little things that we grow to accept and that surround us. Bill writes in his book *Seven Habits of a Healthy Home* what it means to have a place of refuge: "What made it a refuge for us? Open arms. Hugs. A listening ear. Unconditional love. Attention. Our own space. People who adored us with their eyes. People who cared, who were attentive to the little changes in our countenance and voice inflections, who stroked our heads, kissed our cheeks, and fixed our favorite foods at just the right times when we needed a boost. . .

"Home can be for us a refuge, a place to belong and to be loved, a place that accepts us, binds our wounds, and rejuvenates our spirit. Home is people who cuddle us and encourage us, defend us and support us in our grief. It is not a perfect place; we are human, after all. But it is a place with familiar sights and smells, a place where we can let down our guard, set aside our assumed roles, do away with pretenses, and be ourselves. It is a place of grace, of forgiveness. It is a place where memory gathers. In this place, I am welcome. I am safe."[89]

> *"Lately, I have been thinking how comfort is perhaps the ultimate luxury."*
>
> *– Billy Baldwin*

> *"Every house where love abides / And friendship is a guest / Is surely home, and home sweet home / For there the heart can rest."*
>
> *– Henry Van Dyke*

A SAFE HOME OFFERS GRACE

"The ache for home lives in all of us. The safe place where we can go as we are and not be questioned."[90]

You can have a home built like a fortress, but if the people in it are not "safe" people, the home will not feel safe. We surround others with who we are. We make a home with who we are.

Menacing fears such as wars, world dictators, or mass shooters can make us wonder where to find our safe places. Home—a safe place—is something we need more than ever today. Proverbs 18:10 says, "The name of the LORD is a strong tower; the righteous run to it, and they are safe." But there are times when we need God "with skin on"—we need people and places of refuge.

The good news is that we have the privilege of providing such places. We can create a home that is safe for ourselves and for those we love.

Jesus was approachable, and he met people where they were. He was willing to be interrupted, inconvenienced. He said, "Come to me, all you who are weary and heavy-laden." And then he told his disciples that the world would know we were his followers if we loved one another (John 13:35). Who do you call? If you're like me, you have a handful of people, the "safe" ones, the ones who have been through it before. They won't judge. I hope that I'm not perceived as being "too busy" (although I fear I am, as I hear that a lot from friends: "You're so busy.")

Kindness in a home can heal.

Earl and Dorothy Book were our pastors and spiritual mentors many years ago, and Bill and I were their youth pastors. When we arrived to work with them, we were struck by the fact that their church exuded an almost tangible sense of refuge that offered healing from sin and brokenness, paving the way to real transformation. The Books' home was likewise saturated by that sense of grace and safety. Of course, it started with them, personally.

I believe being a safe place means becoming a place where people accept and understand grace—that we all need forgiveness and room to grow, and that we can receive healing from our wounds. I say "becoming," because this is a process not instantly achieved. It means to listen.

There was so much laughter in our conversations with the Books, sitting around their kitchen table after church on Sunday nights. They did not have an uptight sense of doom, of how terrible things were. And they certainly could have—being pastors and hearing so many problems that face people! They had grace instead, and that brought healing.

Listening can heal a broken home, can bring a sense of grace. As a small child, my mother would sometimes hug one of us children, look in our eyes and ask, *"What does it feel like to be you?"* And she really wanted to know. Listening with our hearts as well as our ears allows us to sense grace, to accept grace.

Dallas Willard writes, "How rarely are we ever truly listened to, and how deep is our need to be heard. I wonder how much wrath in human life is a result of not being heard."[91]

Life is messy. We often fail. But the prophet's ancient words comfort us: "This I recall to my mind; therefore I have hope. Through the LORD's mercies we are not consumed, because His compassions fail not. They are new every morning; great is Your faithfulness" (Lamentations 3:21–23).

Listening makes a home feel safe

I hope that I am a "safe" person. That my family and dearest friends can trust me not to hurt them, betray them, or judge them.

Sometimes in the pursuit of being "right," we saints can become hard. Judgmental. Maybe even mean. First, toward ourselves—inwardly whipping ourselves for not doing enough, being enough. *Not good enough.* Then it seeps out toward others, toward our relationships. So: Accept grace for yourself. Relax. Let the conversations in your home be filled with laughter and joy.

A home of protection, of nourishment, of celebration, of comfort, and of grace will heal us.

> *"People give pain, are callous and insensitive, empty and cruel . . . but place heals the hurt, soothes the outrage, fills the terrible vacuum that these human beings make."*
>
> *– Eudora Welty*

Take some time to evaluate your home. Is it a safe place? Ask yourself these questions:

- How can my home offer better protection?
- How can we enhance the power of family dinners or other meals in our home?
- What can we do to celebrate more?
- How does my home currently offer comfort? Is there any way to improve that?
- Is my home a place of grace? First of all, for myself, and then for others?
- Describe an experience where you were a guest at someone's house and you felt welcome and left feeling happier and more whole.
- What did your hosts do to produce that effect?
- Conversely, describe an experience that didn't feel safe. What do you think made it that way?
- Discuss the following quote by Shauna Niequist: *"I think preparing food and feeding people brings nourishment not only to our bodies but to our spirits. Feeding people is a way of loving them, in the same way that feeding ourselves is a way of honoring our own createdness and fragility."*[92]

Evaluate the atmosphere in your home.

- Is there much laughter in your home?
- Is there space for everyone here to be creative?
- If not, what needs to happen to get it there?

Chapter 10

Celebrating the Seasons

"To everything there is a season, A time for every purpose under heaven."

– Ecclesiastes 3:1, NKJV

Today is an exquisite October day: blue skies, warm sunshine. The leaves on the maple tree outside my window are a brilliant orange. Last night it froze, so this weekend I shall reluctantly address my flowers, which look as if they are—well, dying.

On a day like today, summer seems endless. But because I've been around a few seasons, I know it's not. There are abrupt season changes, especially in the small mountain town where we live. It can be winter one day and spring the next. But then there are times when the changes are barely noticeable, and if we're not paying attention, we can miss the signs. A breeze brings a shower of long pine needles to cover the ground behind our house—a sure sign of fall. In late winter, there's a certain feel to the wind, a fresh scent of melting snow from the mountains and the fragrance of earth softening that lets you know that spring is on its way.

At home, the change of season may be imperceptible: both kids are away for sleepovers, and suddenly it's just you and your mate. Or just you. Your college daughter's room seems so very empty, and you realize: Home is different now. You are in a new season, and it's time to learn to celebrate that season.

There is something powerful about celebrating seasons. And celebrating a season doesn't just mean pulling out appropriate décor. Instead, there's a bigger meaning to it.

So why do we do it? Why do we celebrate? It's fun, yes, but it's more than that. Celebrating holidays—holy days—is a way to remind ourselves and our children of timeless touchstones. When the Israelites celebrated Passover, their children asked, "What does this mean?" And the ancient story was retold.

Celebration answers the question of meaning. What does this anniversary mean? This birthday? This special holiday tradition? We gather together, we affirm what we know, and we are glad for it.

Celebrations help create a liturgy of home

There are obvious seasons: spring, summer, fall, and winter. We often decorate our homes accordingly. Flowers in the spring and summer; pumpkins and autumn wreaths in the fall; Christmas garlands and lights in the winter—and of course, all the various holidays that we celebrate in between.

These things add a sense of rhythm, a marking of time, and a reflection of the larger picture of life. They help to create a beautiful liturgy of home. Life can be stressful, with losses and challenges, and taking the time and energy to participate in the seasons pulls us forward, helps us see the joy, helps us heal. Celebrating no matter what is like a continuous thread of joy woven throughout life.

Our lives have seasons too. My children are in the springtime—and some of them in the summer—of their own home lives, creating homes and building occupations and raising children. Metaphorically speaking, I think of springtime as youth: people in their twenties and thirties. Summer represents the forties and fifties; fall is our sixties and over; winter can represent old age.

Just like actual seasons, metaphorical seasons can overlap. Today I will put the high chair back out in the garage, as eighteen-month old Birdie and her three-year-old brother, Conrad, went home yesterday. The double stroller and the wagon of blocks will go back in their spot for another day. It's quiet now, just Papa and me. I am aware that my home—my life—is in its fall. I savor the beauty of where I am, knowing that the only constant is change.

Every season of home has a purpose and sets the stage for the next season. To leave one season is to lose something, but it also means gaining something. So, don't hold back—go ahead, celebrate! Plant the flowers, deck the halls. Celebration makes life worth living.

Celebrating spring

"I must have flowers always and always."

– Claude Monet

There is such hope in spring. There is such hope when we start out as young adults, creating a home or forging a new career. There is such hope when we start out with a marriage: *"I take thee, for better, for worse . . ."* The vows and goals we set take us through all seasons. But we start out, most of all, with hope that planting will bring good, lasting results.

Home has a lot of needs in its springtime. If you are like most, there is the practical, financial need of trying to make it all work. We need money for rent or a mortgage; doctor bills; groceries. We take risks, we try to finish our education, we start a new job.

If babies and children enter our lives, home takes on an even bigger purpose for us. A lot is required of home in the early childhood years. As I look back through my journal when my children were small, I find it was blank for months at a time. Life then was so consumed by the basic demands of feeding and nourishing and training. Much of it seemed like drudgery, but it was a critically important part of life—my children's and mine. Mother Theresa wisely observed, "If you want to change the world, go home and love your family."[93]

The actual season of spring is a welcome one for most of us. Especially if we live in a colder climate, it is beyond wonderful to see crocuses or daffodils poke their heads up out of the earth. New life infuses us with hope, with possibilities. It's time to get outside again. Laura Ingalls Wilder wrote, "Some old-fashioned things like fresh air and sunshine are hard to beat."[94] I agree!

SPRING IDEAS:

> *"It's spring fever. That is what the name of it is. And when you've got it—you want—oh, you don't quite*

know what it is you do want, but it just fairly makes your heart ache, you want it so!"

– Mark Twain

When it comes to decor, many great ideas for all seasons are available—check out Pinterest or stop at a favorite store for inspiration. The best start for spring, though, it to let the fresh air *in.*

- **Freshen up the house.** Do some spring cleaning. Open the windows; wash all the bedding; clean your closets; take inventory.
- **St. Patrick's Day.** Buy a shamrock for your table—even if you're not Irish—and help celebrate this holiday. Revisit the life and real significance of St. Patrick.
- **Easter.** This may the most glorious season of all for many of us. Some of us observe Lent, which leads us into the holy season of Easter. If you haven't done so already, start some of your own traditions to make this time even more meaningful.
- **Gardening and planting.** Plant something new, such as an herb garden. Even if you are in a small apartment, you can find a spot for basil or chives and incorporate them in your cooking.
- **Put out a birdfeeder or a birdbath.** Jesus said, "Consider the birds of the air," and for very good reason. They inspire us to trust our Creator.

"It is Spring again. The earth is like a child that knows poems by heart."

– Rainer Maria Rilke

Celebrating summer

"Summer was our best season: it was sleeping on the back screened porch on cots, or trying to sleep in the tree house; Summer was everything good to eat; it was a thousand colors in a parched landscape."

– *Harper Lee,* To Kill A Mockingbird

Summer brings such a sweet sense of *time* – time that feels suspended. We pretend it will be like this forever as we hang out with the kids in the hammock or play "I spy." We sit in the warm sun; watch the hummingbirds swarm the hanging flower basket. We work in the garden, pulling weeds, and watch flowers and plants – and maybe our children too! – grow. Ah, summer, so lovely with sun tea and reading on the back deck. Barbeques with friends and family. Picking berries that bring the sweetness of homemade jams and pie. Work sometimes takes a back seat in summer, but with the longer days and nights we try to squeeze every drop out of the season.

Still, regardless of how beautiful summer may be, toward the end we become ready for change. The heat may be unrelenting. For us this past summer, there was too much smoke from forest fires. Shrubs and plants seem tired in the dusty earth. There have been too many ice cream cones.

As I look back over the summer of my life, I smile. I enjoyed it so, savoring moments with my family. Summer is a time for watching the stars at night, for long walks early in the morning. Summer is a time to grow – physically as well as metaphorically.

Here are some practical ideas to make the most of summer.

SUMMER IDEAS:

- **Staycations.** Strapped for money and time? Consider a "staycation" instead of traveling far away for a vacation. Take time to see things in your area that other people visit to see—a museum, a special hike. Ride your bike to your own town and pretend you're a tourist.
- **Reunions.** Whether it's with old friends or extended family, summer is a great time to have reunions. It takes organization and planning, but it is well worth the time and energy.

CELEBRATING FALL

> *"Summer is already better, but the best is autumn. It is mature, reasonable and serious, it glows moderately and not frivolously . . . It cools down, clears up, makes you reasonable."*
>
> *– Valentin, Finnish Writer*

Fall can seem like a relief after a frenetic summer. A schedule falls into place once more, the rhythm of work and school and deadlines. Creativity seems to rebound as we have time to breathe again, to think. It is a beautiful time as we watch the colors change in trees and plants. Camus observed that, "Autumn is a second spring when every leaf is a flower." The beauty is all around us, and we stop at roadside stands to sample apple cider and fill our baskets with pears and squash and vegetables.

Fall brings beautiful crisp, cold days. Today, we still have no snow, just crystal-clear blue skies contrasting against the snow-covered mountains with freezing nights. Now is the time for home, for family dinners and Thanksgiving celebrations. The warmth of summer days lingers, but the cold nights warn of the approaching winter. This time of our lives, too, often it seems our seasons overlap. Our children come home; we help parent our grandchildren.

Today the house smells of cinnamon, pumpkin, and apples. The family will be here soon, and I can't wait. While a lot of actual work goes into celebrating Thanksgiving, the best part of all is just being together. We go around the table and ask, "What are you thankful for?"

Then we sing in full harmony, a'capella with all the moving parts: *"Praise God from whom all blessings flow; Praise him all creatures here below; Praise him above, ye heavenly hosts; Praise Father, Son and Holy Ghost. Amen!"*

FALL IDEAS:

- **Family dinners.** Time now for oven dinners or crockpot meals. Weekly planning and shopping help make dinner a time to connect with those we love.
- **Football and soccer games.** Bundle up and get out to enjoy local sports and activities.
- **Harvest festivals.** Many communities have craft fairs in the fall. Stroll through them to get inspired with your own ideas.
- **Thanksgiving.** Christmas has a way of encroaching on Thanksgiving too soon these days, but we can protect this very special holiday when we stop to say, "Thank you, God."

- **If your family is far away**—be proactive. Plan how you will celebrate Thanksgiving. Consider inviting someone over or spend the day volunteering at a local Salvation Army or community outreach.

Celebrating Winter

> *"There ought to be a home for children to come to—and their children—a central place to which they could always bring their joys and sorrows—an old familiar place for them to return to on Sundays and Christmases. An old home ought always to stand like a mother with open arms. It ought to be here waiting for the children to come to it—like homing pigeons."*
>
> – *Bess Streeter Aldrich,* A Lantern in Her Hand

I love the quote above. Oh yes, there ought to be that place! Especially in winter, especially at Christmas. And if you can't go home—or home can't come to you—you can make your own place a warm, welcoming place for yourself. William Morris asked, "Isn't it true that a pleasant house makes winter more poetic, and doesn't winter add to the poetry of a house?"[95]

Even if you live in a warm climate, the earth cools in winter. The days grow shorter, the nights longer, and we tend not to get out as much. We can become more isolated.

We need winter, as much as we resist it. Winter can be a time of silence. A time to ponder what was, what remains. Each season is a precursor of the next, and without winter, there would be no spring with its new life . . . no summer in full bloom . . . no fall with its harvest. Winter is the time when we look back at the previous year. We think about future plantings, what we might do differently. But for this moment, we wait, and we are held in silence. The seed dies, is buried—covered by snow or pelted by rain. There is the sometimes an interminable wait for warmth, for sun again. For new growth, for the thaw. For things to *move.* The poet Shelley asked wistfully, "If winter comes, can spring be far behind?"[96]

Winter is the mature season. It's a time that tests our mettle—a time to live what we know. Winter is a time to read good books, to think. I love what Henry Ford said: "Anyone who stops learning is old, whether at twenty or eighty. Anyone who keeps learning stays young. The greatest thing in life is to keep your mind young."

While cozying up to a fire can be comforting, at times we are reminded that cabin fever is a real thing. Last winter, with its unusual amounts of snow, was a long one for us here in our tiny mountain town. While the snow was beautiful at first against the backdrop of the white twinkly lights of Christmas, the snow got old after we had four feet of snow on our roof. And it kept coming.

Isolation is not healthy for long. It's true as well for the metaphorical winter of our lives. We must be proactive against isolation. Invite people in. Volunteer. Reach out, as we need people.

Winter offers so many reasons to celebrate—chief among them, Christmas. What a gift it is in the winter season that we have Advent . . . and glorious Christmas! And after that, New Year's and cheerful Valentine's Day to lift our spirits.

> *"Winter is the time for comfort, for good food and warmth. For the touch of a friendly hand and for a talk beside the fire. It is the time for home."*
>
> *– Edith Sitwell*

CHRISTMAS IDEAS:

- **Be intentional about what you can do to show love to someone else.** It doesn't take much. Maybe it's denying yourself that latte and dropping the money in the Salvation Army bucket. Or it may be a project that takes a little bit of thought or creativity but is worth it. And if you have children at home—they won't forget being involved in acts of service or mercy.
- **Try to ratchet down the frenetic activity.** Build in quiet evenings at home with Christmas music in the background. Sometimes simplicity is best. Instead of doing everything, delete something.
- **At the same time, don't shut down.** Enjoy the season! Go out and cut down the Christmas tree; drive through neighborhoods to see the lights. The best celebrations are along the way.
- **As life changes, don't be afraid to change your traditions.** Let some go. Add a new one. The idea is to celebrate the wonderful gift of love who is Jesus.
- **Watch your expectations.** Most of our stress comes from inside us—from thinking we must have things just right: the perfect gift, perfect decorations, the perfect Christmas card. Make a budget and stick to it. Ease off the pressure you put on yourself.
- **It's a cliché—but keep Christ in Christmas.** Make room for Jesus in yourself, in your home. How? Just simple awareness. A prayerful walk. Being kind. Listening. Forgiving.

"In the midst of winter, I found there was, with me, an invincible summer. And that makes me happy. For it says that no matter how hard the world pushes against me, within me there's something stronger – something better, pushing right back."

– Albert Camus

Traditions help us celebrate

"Traditions identify us like a fingerprint. They anchor us. If we did not have these particular traditions, we would have others. That is because traditions insist upon themselves: Look around, and you will see them trying to exist everywhere, in everyone's life. Clearly we need them."[97]

– Elizabeth Berg

You may have celebrations that no one else has – they are your own. And that's the fun of it. I know one woman who celebrates the first day of every month at her house with a loved one's favorite dinner. Other traditions are tied to your past: by keeping some traditions that were handed down to you, you can feel closer to your own roots, your own childhood home.

Home is where you don't have to explain traditions. You just know them. You know we sing the Doxology together, and then we have clam chowder and homemade rolls on Christmas Eve. And you know that Dad always reads the Christmas story before we tear into the presents. On Christmas *Eve.* Not Christmas morning. No taking turns, waiting to see what we all got. You just rip into them.

But things change. We grow up. We can't get home, or home changes. If we marry, we become part of another family with its own set of traditions and unwritten expectations. Then you start to make your own traditions, using your own family and others. It takes a while to make your own traditions—to make your own home.

Making and keeping your own traditions is a creative process, and some traditions need to go.

"The past is not dead, it is living in us, and will be alive in the future which we are now helping to make."[98]

Celebrating seasons and observing holidays helps us stay connected to our roots as well as to each other. We need this more than ever, as the world competes nonstop for our attention, our focus. Ron Taffel wrote, *"The truth is that from the day we're born until the day we die, we need to feel held and contained somewhere. We can let go and become independent only when we feel sufficiently connected to other people."*[99]

Staying connected in this world takes discipline, effort, and intention. Leonid Bershidsky writes, "We touch our smart phones—tap, click, swipe—more than 2,500 times a day. That's probably 100 times more often than we touch our partner."[100]

Technology has changed everything, but one way we can counteract technology's pervasive reach is to be proactive in how we use it and how (and when) we don't. Technology can help us to connect, if we learn how to use it and not let it use us. We can:

- Set up a Facetime appointment to connect with friends and family when we want a more intimate chat.

- Call, Facetime, or Skype a family member or good friend who lives far away during a special holiday to help them feel included.
- Occasionally do a group family or friend text to share important news.
- Text-pray prayer needs with a small group. Email works as well, but text is more immediate.

Take some time to consider how you celebrate seasons in your home. Perhaps celebrations at home are important to you; perhaps you don't give it much thought right now. How can celebrations add value and meaning to your home and your life?

Here are some discussion questions:

- What season of "home" are you in now?
- Does your house help facilitate that season?
- If not, how can you make it better for those who live there?
- List ways you can be intentional about celebrating various seasons.
- Consider the possibility that some celebrations need to be deleted, changed, or scaled back.
- What do you like about how you celebrate?
- Try this: Set priorities instead of goals . . . and let them be your guiding principles in the next year.

Our family's favorite tradition: "Cousin Camp" or "Grandkid Camp"

This is a big commitment and not for everyone, but it has added so much enjoyment and meaning to our family life that I must share some tips on how to do it—just in case you'd like to try.

- **Decide on a date.** Determine the length, the theme, and the age group.
- **A theme helps your planning.** Some themes we have used in the past include:

  - ❍ "Star Wars." Scripture: "When I consider the heavens . . ."
  - ❍ Olympics. Scripture: "Run the race to win."
  - ❍ Oregon Trail. Scripture: The exodus story (The children of Israel in the wilderness; the journey of discovery).
  - ❍ Power of Creativity. Scripture: Genesis 1–2, the wonder of creation.
  - ❍ Using your talent. Scripture: parable of the talents.
  - ❍ Family Hall of Fame. Scripture: "The cloud of witnesses."
- **Anticipate. Think things through.** Prepare meals ahead of time and use paper products to make clean-up easier. Give a list to the parents of what they should bring (sleeping bags, etc.). Have crafts available to tie in with the theme. Plan activities, Scripture lessons, and memory verses. Set up a "Camp Store" and make "Camp Bucks" a reward for good behavior and Scripture memory.
- **Involve the kids in the work.** Use sign-up sheets for chores, for meal preparation, and cleanup. They love to help. Let them be creative in decorating and setting the table.
- **Consider one meal when you do "chopped."** Divide into two teams; give them the same ingredients; then taste to see who comes up with the best meal.

OTHER SUGGESTIONS:

- Make T-Shirts for everybody with a logo and their name on it.

- Do a lemonade stand; then divvy up the earnings and go to the Dollar Store.
- Host a scavenger hunt (their all-time favorite!).
- Have a campfire every evening. Tell the stories, and let the kids act out the story.
- Get help if you need it. (Hire an older teen or draft an older cousin to help with the little ones.)

Chapter 11

Sacred Space at Home

"A true home is one of the most sacred of places. It is a sanctuary into which men flee from the world's perils and alarms. It is a resting-place to which at close of day the weary retire to gather new strength for the battle and toils of tomorrow. It is the place where love learns its lessons, where life is schooled into discipline and strength, where character is molded.

Few things we can do in this world are so well worth doing as the making of a beautiful and happy home. He who does this builds a sanctuary for God and opens a fountain of blessing."[101]

While home is a place for our bodies and minds to be restored, it can also be a sacred space where our souls are restored. This is true even despite its ability to be a place where our fears and irritations know no bounds.

When I was a child, our family had a print of William Holman Hunt's depiction of Jesus knocking on a door. It hung on our living room wall, with the quotation below from Revelation 3:20: *"Behold, I stand at the door and knock."*

Similarly, hanging on the wall of our dining room was a small plaque on which was inscribed: *"God is the head of this house – The unseen guest at every meal – The silent listener to every conversation."* That made me gulp occasionally! When I would get into arguments with my siblings or talk back to my parents, it didn't seem to me that Jesus would want to be anywhere near our rowdy bunch.

How do we make sacred space in our homes? It isn't as easy as putting up some religious plaque or an inspirational picture or saying, but we can be intentional about making room in our homes for the sacred.

It starts with you

> *"In solitude, we see more clearly. Alone – in moments of prayer or meditation, or simply in stillness – we breathe more deeply, see more fully, hear more keenly. We notice more, and in the process, we return to what is sacred."*[102]

It starts at ground zero: with us.

How can we have a sense of the sacred if we cannot – at least occasionally – find some solitude somewhere to be at home in the presence of God?

As a young mother, my life seemed impossibly busy. I was consumed with caring for little ones, as well as working part-time editing and writing. I tried to get to a women's Bible study a few times, but one of the kids would be sick; or the babysitter wouldn't show, and I'd wonder, *"What is the point?"* That was when I decided to begin where I was. I would read a Scripture or two on my own at home, or a short devotional from a good book. I tried to be consistent in my reading and then briefly journal a prayer. It wasn't much, it was sporadic, but I began to grow spiritually.

My altar was my kitchen counter, with a Scripture scribbled down on a 3x5 card that I would read and reread when I had a minute. Sometimes my altar was in the laundry room, and as I folded my children's clothes, I would pray for each child. The common became sacred.

We know what we *should* do. With our hectic lives, we are often driven by the urgent. Even so, we can look for and find quiet places to sit down for a moment to take in a Scripture, to invite God into our homes and into our lives. Simply taking a moment to breathe and consider the larger picture and the purpose of our lives will help raise the atmosphere in our homes. We need not be hard on ourselves. The One who loves us most longs simply for our presence too, so that he may speak peace and comfort to us where we are.

Maybe the ultimate sacred space is in our own selves, listening and watching for his presence within. Kitty, a caregiver by occupation, says, "It's not always a 'place' for me. It's where I can find the craved and rare quiet time. It's difficult when you're surrounded by needy people. Often my quiet place is in my van running errands or waiting for one of my clients while she's at an appointment. It's almost like having toddlers again. My prayer is that I don't lose focus of the One who waits for me."

It does help to have a place within our place, as my friend Janis does. She says, "I have a wingback chair in my room that I love. That's my devotion spot and my kneel-and-pray-spot . . . to me, it's holy ground."

Sarah says she loves having an actual closet as a prayer closet. One of her favorites was in a rental house that had a small room under the stairway. "It was great. I think it would be cool to design a house with a prayer closet in the center with just a door and a sky-light! That way at night you could look up at the stars while you talk to God."

Creating a sense of the sacred in your home may take some thought and study. To be intentional about seeking God, we can designate a place, a time. We can light a candle and put on worship music (or good music that elevates the soul). While most of us keep running throughout the day, we can simply sit down for a moment, without distractions. And breathe a prayer: *"Welcome to my home, Lord. Just as it is. Just as I am."*

Ask yourself, "Do I have a place within this house that I can call my own?" If you don't have a bedroom or an office, you can choose a chair in a specific room or a desk in the corner of your bedroom to become that space. It can be a place to put a few of your cherished books, your journal or Bible. In my last house, I had a nook in the loft under the sloping roof. In my present house, I have an office, and I love it. In this room, I have a good chair, my piano, some of my cherished books, and treasured pictures of my family. It is where I keep my desk and computer and write. It is sacred to me. When I walk in, often I will silently invite the Holy Spirit to direct my work that day as I go down my prayer list for family and friends and other needs. My husband's woodworking shop is not only a place where he makes fine handcrafted things for his family; it is also where he prays for our children and grandchildren and the needs of many.

Whatever kind of space you have available, make the effort to create your own place in which to think; a place to dream; a place to hear God. It is said that Susanna Wesley, mother of John and Charles (and many other children), put an apron over her head periodically—a "do not disturb" sign to her family that she was in her place to pray and hear God.

My mother occasionally got in the car and drove down a side road with her Bible and notebook in hand. When she came back, she seemed more content and grounded. She had to be creative to find her spot, but she did. We all have the potential to make room for the sacred in our homes, bringing our own set of priorities into our living space. By what's going on inside of us, we set the tone of our home.

> *"Christ asks for a home in your soul, where he can be at rest with you, where he can talk easily to you, where you and he, alone together, can laugh and be silent and be delighted with one another."*[103]

Guard against intrusions

> *"Did you ever say anything like this to yourself, 'It is so difficult to select a place'? What about the time when you were in love, was it impossible to select a place to meet in? No, it was far from impossible . . . Think how long our Lord has waited for you; you have seen Him in your visions, now pray to Him; get a place, not a mood, but a definite material place and resort to it constantly, and pray to God as His Spirit in you will help you."*[104]

It's been said that if we aim at nothing, we'll hit it every time. I have learned that if I'm to write a book, I need an actual place to write; an actual commitment to do it; an actual deadline to meet. And so it is with the sacred space within our own selves, within our homes. In the early years I described earlier, my actual commitment was an open journal on my kitchen counter, with one Scripture for that day as my day unfolded. My commitment now is different, as is my space. What matters is our aim. To make an actual place is to make an actual commitment.

My friend Celeste said, "Finding the sacred doesn't happen accidentally. It takes intention. We don't stumble into a place of rest. We have to make room for it. Saying no to other things so we can say yes to the important things. I believe the sacred looks different depending upon the season of life we are in."

The world comes at us, but we can be proactive in turning it away. We can turn off the television. We can put phones in their place and refuse to watch mindless, mind-sucking entertainment and social media. Everyone needs some space of his or her own—a place to think, create, read, draw. John Grisham wrote his first novel on a small typewriter crammed between the washer and dryer in his laundry room when he was married with young children and just beginning a law practice. To make something happen, it often takes creativity and thinking outside the box.

Set the Tone for Others

> *"Come, my people, enter your chambers, and shut your doors behind you; hide yourself, as it were, for a little moment."*
>
> *—Isaiah 26:20*

On a recent trip to the Middle East, my husband and I visited many sacred sites. We were told by our guide to dress appropriately, to use a head covering at certain holy places. I wondered, *What makes a place holy?* It seemed, as we visited many such, that a place is made holy by the remembrance of what happened there. Witnesses to Something Big that happened in a place make it sacred—the testament to actual events that shaped and influenced generations.

At the scene in Bethlehem where Jesus was born, I was fascinated as I watched a young mother sitting near the manger scene, holding her young daughter in her arms. Candles were burning as people sang "Silent Night, Holy Night," their voices echoing off the stone walls. I watched candlelight flickering on the mother's face and tears streaming down her cheeks as she held her small daughter. It was a holy place. And she had brought her daughter there, with her.

Sacred space may be about how you approach the smallest, simplest, most ordinary tasks of home life. The daily acts of living—of bathing, breaking bread, sharing drink, caring for our homes—can be part of the sacred, if we see them that way. Listening to the people within our homes; yes, even listening to our own hearts; brings a sense of the sacred. And what is caught is then more easily taught. By our own priorities and convictions, we become contagious to those who are closest to us. We can bring them into our own experience.

Candles are devotional aids. Early Christians lit candles to read texts, but we can also use candles as a symbol of prayer. As Jesus is the light of the world that dispels darkness, so as we light a candle, we remember that he is our Light. His truth lights our pathway.

When we celebrate birthdays, we light candles for every year of our loved one's life so far. It can be a sacred, loving observation as we celebrate those we love and offer gratitude for each year.

Holy places are elusive, but they remind us that some things are sacred, that some things are worth fighting and living and dying for. They are icons. We see through them to the real holy places, our hearts.

Once as a small girl, I got up in the night to go to the bathroom, and I saw my mother kneeling in prayer in the living room, crying out to God for her children. For *me.* She was unaware of my presence, and I tiptoed past, knowing I had witnessed the holy. I never forgot it.

Sacred space is not so much in the outer trappings as in the Spirit who comes to indwell it—to indwell us. God asked David, when David was bent on building a grand house for him: "Would you build a house for me to dwell in? For I have not dwelt in a house since the time that I brought the children of Israel up from Egypt, even to this day, but have moved about in a tent and in a tabernacle. . . And I have been with you wherever you have gone."[d] God reminded David that he was with him, no matter where he was. It is humbling and comforting to know that wherever we are, God wants to dwell with us. And since he dwells in us, we can welcome him into our homes too. A beautiful Scripture from Revelation reminds us that "the dwelling of God is with men, and he will live

---

[d] 2 Samuel 7:5b; 6; 9, NKJV

with them. They will be his people, and God himself will be with them."[e]

At its finest, home has a higher meaning, a holiness about it. It is a place, at its core, to do what matters. To be kind to those who are nearest and dearest to us. It is a place to be honest about who we are. Is it outrageous to suggest that our homes reflect our theology?

Our homes certainly reflect our priorities. Shea Darien wrote, "To make a home into a sanctuary, we must be willing to make room in our hearts for one another's limitations, as well as our gifts. For it is here in this sacred space of the home and family, so brimming with life, so full of every emotion available to our hearts, that we learn what it means to love within all the nuances of an intimate relationship."[105]

We can add meaningful reminders in our home to encourage gratitude and prayerfulness. In an antique hutch, I keep Bill's grandfather's violin, my parents' wedding memento, and pictures of both of our grandparents. It reminds me that I stand on the shoulders of those who have gone on before us.

Bryan Jeffery Leech prayed this eloquent prayer:

> *"Eternal Father of us all, Enter our homes, not as the occupant of a guest room, but as the senior member of each household, that we may live out your love in the most ordinary parts of life.*
>
> *Keep us human as you make us holy. Amen."*[f]

---

[e] Revelation 21:3, NIV
[f] Bryan Jeffery Leech, 1931-2015; Covenant Hymnal

MAKE IT REAL—NOT RELIGIOUS

> *"We all come to prayer with a tangled mass of motives – altruistic and selfish, merciful and hateful, loving and bitter. Frankly, this side of eternity we will never unravel the good from the bad, the pure from the impure. But what I have come to see is that God is big enough to receive us with all our mixture. We do not have to be bright, or pure, or filled with faith, or anything. That is what grace means, and not only are we saved by grace, we live by it as well. And we pray by it."*[106]

At home, we can offer a sense of the holy by honoring the concept of Sabbath. There are times to rest, to unplug and strike the balance of seeing that our home generates a sense of peace and calm.

Writer A.W. Tozer observed, "Wherever we are, God is here. There is no place, there can be no place, where He is not."[107]

Below are practical ideas to bring sacred space to your home. Discuss them and add some of your own ideas.

- **Candles.** When evening comes and it's time for the evening meal, consider lighting candles to soften the mood in your home and add warmth.
- **Cultivate a sense of Sabbath.** Say grace before meals. The words don't need to be eloquent, just heartfelt and honest. There is a time to turn off the television; to stop working. Be sensitive to moments when it's time to just stop and listen.
- **Create your own place.** I like to have pleasant nooks and corners that give a comfortable sense of semi-privacy and yet are not in any way shut off from the rest of the house. Make a place for yourself that is private, yet usable for other things too.
- **Vignettes.** On a dresser or a desk, arrange meaningful prayer reminders of others—pictures, mementos. I have a vignette of photos on my baby grand piano in my office: photos of my and Bill's parents; pictures of some of the homes they made; an array of pictures of my children and grandchildren. I tried to find photos that best represent each of them—their unguarded moments of joy or thoughtfulness. This arrangement says to me that these beautiful children are the fruit of generations of prayer and thoughtfulness, and it reminds me to keep praying and believing for the best for them.
- **Make room for good music.** Martin Luther said, "I wish to see all arts, principally music, in the service

of Him who gave and created them. Music is a fair and glorious gift of God. I would not for the world forego my humble share of music. Singers are never sorrowful, but are merry, and smile through their troubles in song. Music makes people kinder, gentler, more staid and reasonable . . . besides theology, music is the only art capable of affording peace and joy of the heart."[g]

- **Notice beauty around you.** One sun-drenched spring afternoon, I walked along the Metolius River, a beautiful river near our home. A wooden walkway extends down a small stretch of the trail, room for just one. I stood by to allow a woman with a cane walking slowly across the walkway. She smiled apologetically: "I'm sorry I'm so slow!"

  "That's all right," I assured her. "Maybe it's good to be slow, so we can see more." As I waited for her, I realized that slowing down and paying attention to the beauty was exactly what I needed at that moment. I took a deep breath and looked around me. I had been in a hurry to get my two-mile walk in along the river and get back home to work. I remembered Jesus' words to look at the birds of the air; to see the flowers in the field and to remember how he loves us. *Slow down. Look. Listen. Be, don't do.*

  Through the wonders of nature, we can come alive to God's presence. Putting in a birdfeeder or birdbath or working in the garden are ways to bring a

---

[g] www.appleseeds.org/Luther_Music.htm, accessed 3/6/2018

tangible sense of the sacred in your home. As you develop the sense of the sacred in your home, you can keep the soul of your home no matter what season of life you are in; no matter where you go. And in each season of your life, your strength and mooring will come from finding time to be still, to listen to the still small Voice.

There has to be a song –
There are too many dark nights,
too many troublesome days,
too many wearisome miles,

There has to be a song –
To make our burdens bearable,
To make our hopes believable,
To transform our successes into praise,
To release the chains of past defeats,
Somewhere – down deep in a forgotten corner of each man's heart –

There has to be a song –
Like a cool, clear drink of water,
Like the gentle warmth of sunshine,
Like the tender love of a child,
There has to be a song.[108]

Be conscious of the mood your home projects. Does your home help make you (and others who live there) happy?

- What are some creative ways you can find moments of solitude in your home?
- Do you have a place where you can pray?
- If some unpleasant attitudes hold sway at home, what can you do to encourage better ones?

"Your principles have been the music of my life throughout the years of my pilgrimage."

– Psalm 119:54, NLT

Chapter 12

Making a New Home

"This house sheltered us, we spoke, we loved within these walls. That was yesterday. Today we pass on, we see it no more, and we are different, changed in some infinitesimal way. We can never be the same again."

– Daphne du Maurier, Rebecca

Not quite two years ago, our realtor posted a "For Sale" sign in front our house, and Bill and I were filled with mixed emotions. Our house *(a very, very, very fine house!)* had been our family gathering place, and we were reluctant to let it go.

If I were to write the ad for my house, this is how it would be:

For Sale: Warm, comfortable family home. Comes with bacon and huckleberry pancakes on Saturday mornings. Included are beds for everyone who wants to come; a wood fire in the real rock fireplace; an outside fire pit for summer evenings, with good

> *conversations near all these places. The house is used to quality music, and the buyer should also be aware that there is laughter (and some sighing) embedded in the walls.*

Soon prospective buyers began stopping by with their realtors. Bill and I would leave so as not to be in the way, and as we drove out of the driveway, I wondered, *What if my house sells? Who am I, without my house?*

I confess I was in love with the place.

A house helps define us. I carefully kept the house show ready—internally trying to hold loosely, to remind myself that home is not a fixed place (*but oh, it is!*).

And then . . . our house sold.

How can you love something made of wood and stone and glass? Well, you can. We did. We loved the log beams, the way the piano fit in that corner of the loft, the fireplace around which we gathered so many times as family, as friends, as individuals.

We told ourselves that we would make more memories somewhere else, that this was a practical and smart thing to do. And it was. But it meant leaving a place that was filled with memories of laughter and music and good food and celebrations and sleepovers, wedding showers, baby showers, Christmases and Easters. Golf getaways. Annual open houses and spaghetti feasts for wrestlers. Prayer retreats. And maybe the most fun of all, Grandkid Camp.

The stairway was not just stairs: it was a fun slide to go down on sleeping bags. The bonus room was not just Papa's office (although it worked just fine for that purpose, and certainly helped publish a lot of books); it was a place to snuggle up at night and tell stories. My loft office was not just a place where I wrote; it was a place to twirl around in Nana's chair and to play "Thomas the Train."

How many wonderful messes we made in the kitchen! Making huckleberry pies with my granddaughters or decorating sugar cookies with the gang. I bathed many grandbabies in that wonderful kitchen sink.

But things change when we move.

Through time, individuals and families are driven to move to new places, to establish new homes. Some of us stay close to our original homes and connected to our extended families. In tracing my own family's roots, I can see that my father's family—the kin of my grandfather and grandmother Pearson—have deep roots in Sweden and the northern plains of Minnesota, North Dakota, and Montana. My mother's family—at least the Davis branch—are spread throughout America. They were true pioneers, looking for that better place. The Erickson branch of Mother's family settled in Saskatchewan as well as in Minnesota. The Scandinavians seemed to clump together for survival in the new world. The Davises, with their Welsh roots, were more independent and mobile.

I had not given my ancestors much thought until recently, when I decided I wanted to find the places where my grandparents, great-grandparents, and great-great grandparents lived. How I wish I had asked my own parents more questions: *What were your grandparents like? Why did they move when they did? What were their hopes and dreams?*

Perhaps much like us, their great-grandchildren, it was home they wanted.

"All the places we have lived in remain with us, like the pegs in a vast storehouse, on which our memories are hung.

They symbolize all the state of mind through which we have lived, with all their varied shades of feeling."[109]

– Paul Tournier

Making a new home is hard, physical work, like giving birth

Ah, moving.

We all do it at some point—some of us more than others—and it's always a relief when it's over. My husband and I are finally becoming settled in our new home, and how ironic it is to be writing a book about home in what might be the most uprooted time of my life in recent memory. But we are here, finally. Our bed is up. The coffee is ready to go in the morning.

Home is our most intimate place. It is where we nest and make ourselves comfortable. We are creatures of habit: We have a certain chair, a certain spot in the sun. A place for our keys or wooden spoons. Home is our place to sleep, to bathe, to keep our belongings.

Now that I look back on our beloved family house, I see that it was not the home I loved so but the life that I lived there. It had some problems, as houses do. A big consideration was financial. And so, it was time to go.

How do you know when it's time to move?

Maybe your house is the best place for you right now, due to location or financial constraints, but sooner or later, its function will change as your life changes. And change it will, as change is the only thing we can count on. The hard question to ask is, *Is my present house making my life work? Or do we need to make a change? And would moving help, or should we stay here?*

I write from my new office, which gets the morning sun. I am surrounded by my beloved books, which came with me. It is a cheerful room. On my piano is a kaleidoscope of family photos that I brought with me. I fiercely needed them. How much love can the top of a piano hold? A lot.

Sitting here, I'm reminded of the constant need to let go of places while living the paradox of holding on to what's important. You must have a place in order to leave. Place launches you; helps you grow. Even nature teaches us this, as we watch baby birds leave their nest. We can't reach our full potential if we don't leave, sometime. It is what we must do—more than once, in most cases. Leaving home when you are young is one thing. It is another to leave when you are older, when you must leave one home to make another. Loss happens *to* all of us; it is not our choice. We may need to move because of the death of a loved one. A reversal of health. A divorce we didn't want. A job change.

> *"Home wasn't a set house, or a single town on a map. It was wherever the people who loved you were, whenever you were together. Not a place, but a moment, and then another, building on each other like bricks to create a solid shelter that you take with you for your entire life, wherever you may go."*[110]

Feeling at Home in a Changing World

Shortly after we moved to our new house, we were on a weekend getaway to the Oregon coast. Although we could have stayed one more day, Bill said, "I want to go *home.*" I agreed—I wanted home too. Life had been hectic with our recent move, and we wanted the comfort of our own place. Off we sped toward home, east over the mountains, over Santiam Pass. We zipped right past the Camp Sherman turnoff—past our Camp Sherman home—and arrived here, in Sisters. But it felt temporary.

We walked into the house with our bags to unpack, and I thought, *This house is too noisy.* I was not used to the sound of a heat pump. I opened the window and heard the sound of traffic. In our Camp Sherman house, I was used to hearing the sounds of crickets and birds, or coyotes and owls through my open window.

I sat at my new kitchen table, making lists, trying to make the house a home. The move was harder than I thought it would be. I felt lost without my river walks, and Bill felt lost without his woodshop.

But now, a year out, I have found a new walk through the woods behind our house. Bill has a new woodworking shop, even better than the last one. We just had Thanksgiving, and our oldest grandson, Will, was here along with the rest of the family. When he came down to a breakfast of bacon and Papa's strawberry waffles, he confessed, "I was afraid to come here because Camp Sherman was so special, and it's gone. Now it's here again! Your home is where you are."

> *"Do not remember the former things, nor consider the things of old. Behold, I will do a new thing, now*

it shall spring forth; shall you not know it? I will even make a road in the wilderness and rivers in the desert."

–Isaiah 43:18–19

Focus on the positive

Letting go is hard work. Never say that it is not. But letting go is necessary to live a full, joy-filled life and to thrive where you are. How do folks get used to a new place? The not-so-wonderful place that may be a "downsizer"? I watched Bill's father bravely embrace his new place at Whispering Winds, a retirement home, when he was age ninety-five. He was so courageous! And my mother, selling her beloved new home to move to an apartment. She did it with such cheer and grace.

I am realizing that maybe one of the most important parts of life is learning how to let go. Not letting go of love—never that! Knowing when, and how, and what to keep. I tell myself, "Have courage. It takes courage to leave the old, to embrace the new. Be the home now for Bill, for yourself. Slow down a bit. Breathe."

How essential it is to focus on the positive. Our youngest daughter, Amy, a new mother with an infant, is delighted that we live closer to her now. I must admit it is more convenient to live in town than eighteen miles away, especially on icy roads in the winter. We can walk or ride our bikes to the store, which is great exercise for us. Living here, we are more readily available to some of our family; we are closer to our church. The move has also helped us, financially.

In order to make a successful transition to a new home, how important it is to rehearse the positive aspects of the move in order to not get stuck in longing for the past.

To embrace a new home, you must let go of:

- Wanting something else—*"I wish I had that home."*
- Regrets—*"Why did we move from there?"*
- A sense of unfulfilled perfection— *"My closet should be cleaner. My desk or office should be more organized."* Maybe it's good enough.
- Comparison with others— *"Her home looks so great, and mine . . ."*
- Appearance—*"My home is a reflection of me, and it's not so great!"*

When someone in your home becomes a memory

It's an odd thing, death. I never get used to it. You would think I would have, by now. My uncles: Bernhard, Hub, Tony, Kenny, Ray, Gordon. My aunts: Evelyn, Emma. My grandparents, Gabriel and Henney. My grandmother, Maude Ann. My beloved mother, Harriet, and my father, Gunder. I say their names, because they are *my* people.

Recently, we had another death in the family. My mother-in-law, Betty, joined her husband, Harold, in the presence of God. She had just turned ninety-three. A long life, yes. Well lived, yes. But still . . . it was over. We knew it was going to happen; we had hospice in place. We all prayed for mercy, and yet when death came, we were startled, somewhat stunned. "Are you all right?" we ask, just to make sure of each other. "You still there? Good. So am I." Tears flow.

My son Eric called, asking me, "What was Grandma's favorite dinner?"

"Well, I guess it would be pot roast . . . with carrots, mashed potatoes, and gravy. And pie for dessert. With ice cream." On his lunch hour he went to the store, got the ingredients, and we had Mom's "Sunday dinner" that Tuesday night.

After dinner we sat around Eric and Carly's table and shared good memories. Something big happens to a family when a mother dies. Even though she was old and couldn't remember anyone's names; even if she couldn't make her special pies and recipes anymore. She was a homemaker, and she fiercely held the hearts of us, her family, who represented her home.

Lasting influences

Our parents give us powerful, life-shaping material that affects our lives; and we likewise hand down powerful, life-shaping material to our own children. This isn't just metaphor; it's a scientific reality.

A research team in the Netherlands discovered that cells from both sons and daughters can escape from the uterus and spread through a mother's body. Fetal cells don't just drift passively, and studies show that fetal cells that end up in the heart develop into cardiac tissue. "They're becoming beating heart cells," said Dr. J. Lee Nelson. A new study suggests that women almost always acquire fetal cells each time they are pregnant. In later years, the cells may disappear, but sometimes, the cells settle in for a lifetime.[111] Maybe this is why losing a mother is so painful. You lose part of yourself.

And on the other side, our children are always with us. Have you ever had the sensation that while your child is out on the basketball court, or giving a speech, or playing at a concert, or making a long trip somewhere, your heart is literally with them? Even if they're all grown up with a responsible job and education, or if they are parents themselves, you still feel their losses and their gains. The adage that having a child means that your heart is just walking around out there may, in fact, be true.

Going home

"It is not down in any map. True places never are."

– Herman Melville

Not long ago my husband and I drove home to Montana, this time with a couple of our grandboys, eager to show them the home place. As we got closer, I drank in the view—the rolling plains, the majestic Rockies off to the west.

Early the next morning, I walked down the familiar graveled road past the farmhouse that is now my brother Dan's beloved home. The air was filled with the meadowlark's song. Memories of being at home cascaded over me, as sure as the meadowlarks' exquisite music: my mother's laughter; my father's halting, gentle voice, still with a Swedish lilt. Memories of playing with my siblings, practicing the piano, being at the country school. Everything was here, and now it was gone, like a brief, shining moment.

We visited all the old places, climbing in the barn, walking the country roads. And as the time came for us to leave a couple of days later, I realized I was ready to leave. I felt homesick, missing my Oregon home. I wondered, someday, would my grown-up children make pilgrimages back to our home, and would they remember good times?

> *"Home was not the place where you were born but the place you created yourself, where you did not need to explain, where you finally became what you were."*[112]

Now as I try to feel at home in my new place, I remind myself that it will take time and effort. I am getting to know my new neighbors. But there's a bigger message here. Much of life is a metaphor, and the ordinary contains profound. So it is with our homes. We can learn much wisdom from them as we look a little deeper and discover unexpected truth. Home is a sacred place; even if it's just for one person.

I'm aware that I'm having a Big Birthday next week, and I keep telling myself that it's just a number. But I'm also aware that winter is a time for realism and humility, and winter is upon me.

What is that emotion that keeps sneaking around the edges of my soul? It took me awhile to identify it, but now I know: *Fear*. That old sneak! He's bugged me before: tormented me when as a young mom I was home alone with four little boys as my husband was on missions trips overseas. Then later, taunted me as I was trying to write my first book ("You can't write a book!") or sent silent messages that there was no way I could speak to people and make a difference. Fear let me know that it was crazy to adopt a child from another country and patch her into our home.

And now here he comes again, reminding me that my best homes are behind me—and to just get used to it. Fear takes strange disguises sometimes: Dismay because I can't find cute shoes that don't hurt. Consternation because the scale doesn't budge no matter what I do. I'm aware that all the stretches and exercises in the world won't reverse aging, although it can delay it.

But this morning my sweet husband had a French roast coffee waiting for me. I walked down the hallway of my home and stopped to look at the pictures of my beloved, large, and growing family. An irresistible rush of joy washed over me: *I have had such a great life!* I think back over time and realize that what defeated fear in the past was God's Word. *The Lord is my light and my salvation. Whom shall I fear? I can do all things through Christ who strengthens me. He who began a good work in me will complete it.*

Today I needed a fresh word from the Word, and here it came: *"She is not afraid of snow for her household, for all her household is clothed with scarlet. She makes tapestry for herself . . ."*[h] It speaks profoundly to me at this place in my life.

As I look back, I have known sorrow. I have known disappointment, and I know the lingering taste of regret. But transcending all of it, I know unbounded joy. I'm held, safely covered in God's hands. Fear was wrong about all of the things he tried to worry me about.

I'm a grateful woman. Grateful for all my life. All of it. Even for the fear, because it drove me to depend on God. And I'm not afraid of winter, for my household is covered.

Once in a while, in this new place, I am tempted to long for my former home, where I could open my window wide at night to hear the wind sighing through the

---

[h] Proverbs 31:21–22

pine trees and the coyotes' distant howl. Where at first light, birdsong filled the air, awakening me.

But perhaps the home I am really longing for is heaven, where all is made plain and the story ends, happily ever after. The loved ones find each other after all the distance; the many wrongs are righted. The messy, hard places are smoothed out, and all is redeemed. No more anxiously looking out the window, praying for everyone to come home.

Because, finally, everyone is home. Safely home.

> *"The sweetest thing in all my life has been the longing – to reach the Mountain, to find the place where all the beauty came from . . . my country, the place where I ought to have been born. Do you think it all meant nothing, all the longing? The longing for home? For indeed it now feels not like going, but like going back."*[113]

Reflect on your most recent move. What was easy about it, and what was hard? List ways that have helped you make your new home "yours."

Discuss these questions:

- How are you creating a home with a sense of permanence in a changing world?
- Does your current house fit your current needs?
- Is it possible that you can work with what you have?
- Discuss the consequences of various moves you have made and how they impacted you.

FURTHER INSIGHTS:

- Embrace the home you have right now, as it is only a brief stop. Savor it. It will change.
- Be content where you are while you keep a vision of the home that's possible for you. Dreams are powerful, and you can always find ways to improve the function of your home.
- Understand that the function of your home will change in various stages of life. Understand and own the core purpose of your home.
- Relationships within your home are what make it beautiful. Your home exists to serve those in it. There's a subtle difference between serving your home and letting your home serve you.
- Keep the Big Picture of what your home can be—and invite God's presence there. Your home can be an anchor for you, for your family, and the generations that will come from you.

Prayer:

Thank you, Father, for the metaphors that you place in our lives. What we long for is home—a place of security and peace and loving acceptance. The homes we establish on this earth, as wonderful as they are, are transient and changing. But they are only a poor reflection of the amazing home you offer us—your very eternal presence in our lives!

You also offer us a home in heavens, not made with hands. Come into our lives, Lord Jesus. We welcome you and rejoice in knowing you as our eternal home. In Christ's name, amen.

Acknowledgments

So much goes into the making of a book.

Mostly, a book comes out of a life. I'm grateful for mine, with all its imperfections and gifts; and I'm grateful to my parents for creating unforgettable images of a childhood home.

Thank you to my husband Bill, for partnering with me in the lifelong quest of Home. Bill's creativity and commitment has helped make a sheltering place for our family, ourselves, and others. But it takes a village to make a home, and I'm thankful for extended family and friends who inspire me with their vision of home.

The Deep River Team has made my heart-and-soul book a joyous experience. Being on the author end of this publishing venture has given me a delightful view of my publishing team as the true professionals they are who give utmost care and support to their authors. Heartfelt thanks to Bill Carmichael, Andy Carmichael, Tamara Barnet, Bev Tucker, and Alexis Miller.

Years ago, Gwendolyn Babbitt illustrated my column "The Deeper Life" in *Virtue Magazine,* and I'm so pleased to have a Gwendolyn Babbitt illustration on my new book. Thanks, as well, go to Jason Enterline for the cover design.

To my extraordinary editor, Rachel Starr Thomson: You are amazing! Thank you for helping to corral my sometimes-meandering words to clarify my message of Home.

About the Author

Nancie Carmichael has been involved in writing and publishing for many years, including at *Virtue Magazine* and *Christian Parenting Today Magazine,* where she was co-publisher with her husband, Bill. She has edited and written many articles, Bible studies, and magazine columns.

The Unexpected Power of Home is Nancie's tenth book. Her other nine include two coauthored with Bill: *Lord, Bless My Child* and *Lord, Bless this Marriage*. Among her most treasured solo endeavors are *Selah: Your Moment to Stop, Think, and Step into Your Future* and *Surviving One Bad Year*. Bill and Nancie now own a book publishing company in Sisters, Deep River Books. Nancie has spoken in many places throughout North America and served on various boards.

Nancie graduated with her MA in Spiritual Formation from George Fox Evangelical Seminary and, in addition to writing, does some counseling through Westside Church in Bend, Oregon. Nancie is also a licensed minister with the Oregon Ministry Network.

Nancie will tell you her greatest joy is her family—her husband Bill, five married children, and fourteen grandchildren. Her favorite thing to do is walk along the

Metolius River or find a beautiful path through the woods near her home in Sisters, Oregon.

Contact the Author

www.nanciecarmichael.com

Facebook.com/nancie.carmichael

Twitter: @CarmNancie

Endnotes

Chapter 1

1. Robert Fulgham, *All I Really Needed to Know I learned in Kindergarten,* (Ballantine Books, 2004)
2. Rafe Esquith, *Real Talk for Real Teachers:* quoting Dr. Seuss (New York: Penguin/Random House, 2014)
3. William Morris, English designer & poet, 1834–1896
4. Dr. Tim Clinton and Dr. Gary Sibcy, quoting Fran Stott in *Attachments: Why You Love, Feel, and Act the Way You Do* (Nashville: Thomas Nelson, 2002), 104
5. Jeffrey A. Wands, *Knock and the Door Will Open: 6 Keys to Mastering the Art of Living,* (Atria Books, 2010)
6. H. Jayne Faulkner, *The Place of Belonging* (Sisters, Oregon: Deep River Books Publishing, 2010)
7. Wallace Stegner, *Angle of Repose* (New York: Penguin, 1992)

Chapter 2

8. Willa Cather, *Lucy Gayheart,* (New York: Alfred A Knopf, 1935)
9. Paul Tournier, *A Place for You* (New York: Harper & Row Publishers, 1968), p. 136
10. Genesis 12:1, NKJV, Thomas Nelson, 1999

11. http://native-american-indian-facts.com/Famous-Native-American/Facts/Squanto-Facts. Accessed 9-21-2017
12. Martin Dugard, *Farther Than Any Man – The Rise and Fall of Captain James Cook;* (New York: Pocket Books of Simon & Schuster, Inc., 2001)
13. Lillian Schlissel, *Women's Diaries of the Westward Journey* (1982), p. 13
14. Ibid., p. 28
15. *www.frontiertrails.com*
16. Ron Taffel, Ph.D, and Melinda Bau, *Parenting by Heart: How to Stay Connected to Your child in a Disconnected World* (DaCapo Press, 2002)
17. Ari Berk, *Death Watch* (New York: Simon & Schuster, 2011), p. 266
18. Beth Hoffman, *Looking for Me* (New York: Penguin/Random House, 2013)

Chapter 3

19. William Kittredge, *Hole in the Sky* (New York: Alfred P. Knopf, 1992)
20. pseudonym
21. Maya Angelou, *Letter to My Daughter,* (New York: Random House, 2002)
22. Genesis chapters 37–50
23. C. S. Lewis, quoted in *Doubleday Christian Quotation Collection,* Hannah Ward and Jennifer Wild, eds. (New York: Doubleday, 1998), 286
24. Genesis 1:2b, NKJV, 1999
25. Josh Gates, *Destination Truth: Memoirs of a Monster Hunger,* (New York: Simon & Schuster, Gallery Books, 2011)
26. John Argue, *Homesick,* quoted in *Where the Heart Is; A Celebration of Home.* Ed. by Julienne Bennette and Mimi

Lueggermann, (Berkeley, California, Wildcat Canyon Press, 1995), p. 136

27. Michele Jaffe, *Ghost Flower: First Edition* (New York: Penguin Group, 2012)

Chapter 4

28. Frederick Buechner, *The Sacred Journey,* (San Francisco: Harper Collins, 1982), p. 11
29. Ben Robertson; *Red Hills and Cotton* (University of S. Carolina Press, 1983)
30. Homelessness Statistics, www.futureinhumanity.org, accessed 6-14-17
31. Practical things to do for the homeless:
    - Keep a few granola bars in your car to give the homeless
    - Buy a few fast-food gift cards that you can hand out
    - In cold weather, keep a bag of extra gloves and socks
    - Support you local shelter with food and clothing and supplies
32. Meghan Daum, *Life Would Be Perfect If I Lived in That House* (Picador, 2015)
33. Pro. 24:3–4, NKJV, Thomas Nelson, 1999
34. Vera Nazarian, *The Perpetual Calendar of Inspiration,* (Spirit Publisher, 2010)
35. Ralph Waldo Emerson, quoted in *Treasure Chest,* p. 93
36. 1 Timothy 6:6, NKJV, Thomas Nelson, 1999
37. Shakespeare, *Hamlet,* quoted in *Bartlett's Familiar Quotations,* 16th Ed., John Bartlett and Justin Kaplan, eds. (Boston: Little, Brown, 1992), p. 194
38. Rudyard Kipling, *Our Lady of the Snows,* quoted in Barlett's Familiar Quotations, 16th ed., John Bartlett and Justin Kaplan, eds. (Boston: Little, Brown, 1992), p. 592

39. Dorothy H. Rath, *The Treasure Chest* (New York: HarperCollins, 1995), p. 92

Chapter 5

40. Lev Grossman, *The Magicians,* (New York: Penguin, 2010)
41. Elizabeth Eulby, *Better Off Friends* (Scholastic Inc., 2015)
42. Brother Lawrence, *Practicing the Presence of God* (Grand Rapids, Mi.: Baker Books, 1989)
43. Suzanne Woods Fisher, *The Keeper,* (Revell: 2012)
44. Salmon Rushdie, *Imaginary Homelands: Essays and Criticism* 1981-1991
45. Psalm 84:5, NKJV, Thomas Nelson, 1999

Chapter 6

46. 2 Kings 4, NKJV, Thomas Nelson, 1999
47. Samuel Butler, *The Way of All Flesh,* (ReadaClassic.com, 2010)
48. Richard Rohr, *Falling Upward,* (San Francisco: Jossey-Bass, 2011)
49. Dale Carnegie, *How to Win Friends and Influence People,* (New York: Simon & Schuster, 1936)
50. Cheryl Mendelson, *Home Comforts* (Scribner, 2005) p. 20
51. *Maud's Pear Conserve.* Here it is, from a note scribbled on a blank card by my mother, Harriet:

    4 lbs. ripe pears, cut quite fine.

    1 No. 25 can sliced pineapple (or drained crushed)

    1 med. size bottle of maraschino cherries

    4 lbs. sugar, approximately

    Drain & dice pineapple and add to pears. Put in cherries (diced) with the syrup. Measure fruit into large kettle. Add 3/4 C. sugar for each C. fruit. Cook *gently* to a runny or thick consistency, as you prefer.

52. Ursula K. LeGuin, *Voices,* (San Diego, Ca.: Harcourt, 2006)

53. Augustine of Hippo, *Confessions of St. Augustine,* Book 1, ch. 5 (New York: Penguin Books, 1963).
54. Donna Smallin, *Clear the Clutter, Find Happiness* (North Adams, MA, 2014), p. 107
55. Bill & Nancie Carmichael, *Lord Bless My Child – Praying for the Character of God in your Child* (Sisters, Oregon: Deep River Books, 2011)
56. Marie Kondo, *The Life-Changing Magic of Tidying Up: The Japanese Art of De-cluttering and Organizing,* (Berkely, Ca.: Ten Speed Press, 2014)
57. AARP, *The Magazine*/June/July 2017, p 14
58. Peter Walsh quoted in *To Lose Weight, Put Your Home on a Diet,* by Neil Wertheimer with Callan Mathis in AARP *The Magazine,* June/July 2017
59. From a Blog by Colleen Madsen, *365 Less Things,* www.becomingminimalist.com/decluttering-principles, accessed 8-23-2017
60. Joanna Gaines in *The Magnolia Journal,* Spring 2017, p. 87
61. William Wordsworth, *Sonnet;* Quoted in One Hundred and One Famous Poems; (Contemporary Books, Inc., Chicago, Ill.), p. 64
62. http://BostonGlobe.com/metro/2017/04-04/baby-boomers-are-downsizing-and-kids-won't-take-family-heirlooms/
63. from www.cleanmama.net

Chapter 7

64. David M. Foley, quoted in *Timberframe* by Tedd Benson (The Taunton Press, Newtown, CT, 1999), p. 186
65. University Students to design custom tiny home, by Rachel Rippetoe, *The Eugene Register-Guard;* Aug. 6, 2017
66. *Luxury Dream Homes* (Published by Home Planners, LLC, Tucson, Az., 2001) p. 6
67. Alexandra Stoddard, *Creating A Beautiful Home;* (Avon Books, New York, New York, 1992), p.17,18

68. Laura Ingalls Wilder from *Words from the Fearless Heart* Stephen W. Hines, ed., (Nashville: Thomas Nelson, 1995), p. 100
69. Golden rule of *The Beauty of Life,* 1880's (William Morris, 1834-1896)
70. Prov. 14:1, NKJV, Thomas Nelson, 1999
71. Meghan Daum, *Life Would be Perfect if I Lived in That House,* (New York: Alfred A. Knopf, 2010)

Chapter 8

72. Frederick Waterman, *Moments Together for Growing Closer to God* (Regal, 2003)
73. Shauna Niequest, from Willow Creek TV (August 25, 2013)
74. Proverbs 11:17, The Living Bible, Tyndale, 1971
75. Gerrit S. Dawson, *Feasts in the Desert and Other Unlikely Places,* (Weavings, J/F, 1994)
76. Matthew 25:31-46
77. Hebrews 13:2, NKJV, Thomas Nelson, 1999
78. Ellen Baker, *Keeping the House* (New York: Random House, 2008) Chapter header quote from *Popular Home Decorations,* 1940

Chapter 9

79. Karen L. Tornberg, quoted in *Seven Habits of a Healthy Home* by Bill Carmichael (Sisters, Oregon: VMI Publishers, 1997)
80. Frederick Buechner, *Beyond Words, Daily Readings in the ABC's of Faith;* (HarperSanFranciso, 05/04)
81. Shauna Niequist, *Bread and Wine; A Love Letter to Life Around the Table with Recipes;* (Grand Rapids: Zondervan, 2013)
82. www.health.com, accessed 9-2-2017
83. https://thefamilydinnerproject.org/resources/faq, accessed 10-9-2017
84. Ibid.

85. Ibid.
86. John 14:2, NKJV, Thomas Nelson 1999
87. Matthew 14:13-21
88. Billy Baldwin, quoted in *Home: A Short History of an Idea* by Witold Rybczynski (New York: Penguin books, 1986), 101
89. Bill Carmichael, *Seven Habits of a Healthy Home,* (Sisters, Oregon: VMI Publishers, 1997), p. 17,18
90. Maya Angelou, *All God's Children Need Traveling Shoes,* (New York: Random House, 1986)
91. Dallas Willard, *Spirit of the Disciplines;* Harper & Row, San Francisco, 1988; p. 164
92. Shauna Niequist, *Bittersweet: Thoughts on Change, Grace, and Learning the Hard Way* (Grand Rapids: Zondervan, 2013)

Chapter 10

93. Mother Theresa, *A Simple Path,* (Ballantine Books, 1995)
94. Laura Ingalls Wilder, Ed. by Stephen W. Hines, *Farm Journalist: Writing from the Ozarks;* (University of Missouri, 2008)
95. William Morris, English clergyman and poet; 1834-96
96. Percy Bysshe Shelley, *Ode to the West Wind,* (Chicago: 101 Famous Poems, Contemporary Books, Inc. 1958), p. 20
97. Elizabeth Berg, quoted in *Seven Habits of a Healthy Home* by Bill Carmichael (Sisters, Oregon: VMI Publishers, 1997), p. 130
98. William Morris, English clergyman and poet; 1834-96
99. Ron Taffel, quoted in *Seven Habits of a Healthy Home* by Bill Carmichael (Sisters, Oregon: VMI Publishers, 1997), p. 139
100. Leonid Bershidsky, founder of slon.ru, writing for Bloomberg News, September 5, 2017

Chapter 11

101. James Russell Miller, *Secrets of a Happy Home Life* (Bottom of the Hill Publishing, 2011)

102. Katina Kenison, *Why You Must Have Time Alone* (Opraph.com-accessed 12/3/2017, Harpo Productions, 2017)

103. Caryll Houselander, *This War Is the Passion,* (Ave Maria Press, 2008)

104. Oswald Chambers, *Christian Discipline;* Ed. by Harry Ver-Ploegh, Vol. 2 (Nashville: Oliver Nelson, division of Thomas Nelson) 1989

105. Shea Darian, *Sanctuaries of Childhood: Nurturing a Child's Spiritual Life,* (Gilead Press, 2001)

106. Richard Foster, *Prayer, Finding the Heart's True Home* (San Francisco: HarperSanFrancisco, 1992)

107. A. W. Tozer, *The Pursuit of God* (Aneko Press, updated from 1948 ed.) chapter 5

108. Robert Benson, *There Has to be a Song,* (from *New Songs of Inspiration #7,* 1976)

Chapter 12

109. Paul Tournier, taken from *Treasures of Inspiration* (Fort Worth, Tex.: Brownlow, 1992).

110. Sarah Dresser, *What Happened to Goodbye* (Viking Books for Young Readers, 2011)

111. "A Pregnancy Souvenir: Cells That Are Not Your Own," by Carl Zimmer, Sept. 10, 2015, *New York Times*

112. Dermot Bolger, (James A. Michener) *The Journey Home* (University of Texas Press, 2008)

113. C. S. Lewis, *Till We Have Faces,* (Orlando, FL: Harcourt, 1956), 75,76